The Fight for Welsh Freedom

I'm chwaer Ceridwen

GWYNFOR EVANS

The Fight for

Welsh

Freedom

y Lolfa

First impression: 2000
Second impression: 2002
Third impression 2006
© Copyright Gwynfor Evans and Y Lolfa Cyf., 2000

Cover design: Ceri Jones
Cover photograph: Marian Delyth

Thanks to Heini Gruffudd and
the National Library of Wales for the photographs.

ISBN: 0 86243 515 3

Printed and published in Wales by:
Y Lolfa Cyf., Talybont, Ceredigion SY24 5AP
e-mail ylolfa@ylolfa.com
internet www.ylolfa.com
phone +44 (0)1970 832 304
fax 832 782

Contents

Foreword	7
Caradog and the Roman Invasion	9
Germanising Britain Begins	11
The Welsh Kingdoms of the Old North	12
Cymru (Wales) is Born	13
A Celtic Confraternity	14
Cymru is a Nation, Christian and Cultured	17
Arthur Halts the Germanic Advance	19
Heirs to Romano-British Civilisation	21
Reinvigoration of Welsh Life	25
Codification of Welsh Law in the Welsh Language	27
Black Pagans and Golden Literature	29
A United Wales	31
The Norman Invasion	32
Normans on the Rampage	34
The Cymry Fight Back	35
Freedom is Established	37
Princess Gwenllïan Killed in Battle	38
The Rule of the Great Princes	40
Prince Owain Gwynedd	41
Battle of the Berwyn	44
Rhys ap Gruffudd Restores Welsh Rule Throughout the South	47
Gerald the Welshman, Three-quarters Norman	51
The Fight for Welsh Church Freedom	53
European Fame of the Glorious King Arthur	56
Prince Llywelyn Fawr (the Great)	57
Prince Llywelyn ap Gruffudd Fights to the Death	62
Llywelyn is Recognised as Prince of Wales	64
Ah God, that the Sea would Cover the Land	68
Edward I's Wales	72
The Risings of Madog and Llywelyn Bren	74
Owain of the Red Hand, the Deliverer	78
Owain Glyndŵr's War of Liberation	81
Owain Crowned Prince of Wales	84

Welsh Confidence Remains	91
The Fateful Battle of Bosworth Field	96
A Pyrrhic Victory for the Welsh	97
For Ever and Henceforth Incorporated and Annexed	99
Welsh Self-confidence Fades	101
Aristocrats and Squirearchy Turn their Backs on their Nation	102
The Struggle of the Cultural Nationalists	104
A Literate Nation	105
The Chartist 'Silurian Republic'	110
The Children of Rebecca	111
'The Treason of the Blue Books'	114
Michael D. Jones	117
The Patagonian Venture	119
Tom Ellis, Lloyd George and Liberal Domination	122
The Short-term Development of Political Nationalism	125
The Labour Party, Believing in Self-government, Takes Over	128
The Formation of Plaid Cymru, The Party of Wales	131
The Leadership of Saunders Lewis	132
The Variety of Nationalisms	134
Welsh Language Programmes Threat to the English Language	135
The Fire in Llŷn	137
The Influence of D.J. and Noëlle Davies	139
Fighting for the National Language	142
Welsh Nationalism Here to Stay	144
Defending Welsh Land	145
Campaign for a Welsh Parliament	145
Defending the Tryweryn Valley	148
Stumbling Towards Self-government in Scotland and Wales	156
New Leadership in Difficult Circumstances	160
Awakening the National Consciousness	162
Plaid Cymru the Second Party, Ahead of Liberals and Tories	166
Wales and the European Union	167
Labour Party Members Warm to Wales	169
A Quiet Revolution	172
The Range of Plaid Cymru's Success	174
On the Threshold of National Freedom	175

Foreword

AN IMPRESSIVE FEATURE in the growth of Welsh national consciousness during the last generation has been the rise of a distinguished school of historians who have enabled splendid teachers to put the youth and children of Wales in possession of the nation's past. Until recently the schools ignored Welsh history, which was despised by great numbers of Labour and Tory politicians. Neil Kinnock (leader of the British Labour Party for nine years) for instance, who called himself a 'unionist', stated in a radio programme broadcast in the United States that 'between the mid-sixteenth century and the mid-eighteenth century Wales had practically no history at all, and even before that it was the history of rural brigands who have been ennobled by being called princes'. Today few, even among the most extreme of British nationalists, would venture to insult the national memory of Wales as coarsely as that.

As loyalty to their nation has increased among the people of Cymru (Wales), so opposition has burgeoned to the policy pursued in London for centuries of assimilating Wales to form a phantom nation, known after the union of Scotland with England (incorporating Wales) as Britain. The day is approaching when England will be compelled to abandon this policy. Cymru will then live fully as a free nation.

Gwynfor Evans

Caradog and the Roman Invasion

When the Romans invaded Cymru (Wales), the language and culture of Wales and most of Ynys Prydain (the Isle of Britain) were Celtic. The island's peoples were related to the Celtic peoples who had dominated Europe, from Galatia to Galicia, from the sixth to the third century BC. They were subjugated by the growing Roman Empire. Julius Caesar himself led the conquest of Gaul where, as in other conquered Celtic lands, the Celtic languages and culture were Romanized out of existence.

Although Julius Caesar made two large-scale raids on Celtic Britain, a century passed before a Roman army of forty thousand men conquered and occupied the south-eastern British kingdom which had been governed by Cynfelin (Cunobelinus – Shakespeare's Cymbeline). After the defeat, his son Caradog (Caratacus), who already had a high military reputation, led the continuing resistance, using guerrilla tactics of which he was a master. He made his base among the Silurians of south-eastern Wales. Caradog can be regarded as the first Welsh king. Under his leadership the Silurians, who were famed for their military

Caradog

prowess, harried the Romans and made two major attacks on the Roman province. With every success, and there were many, Caradog's standing increased. As the recognized leader of the British defence he switched from the land of the Silurians to mid-Wales to organise the defence there. His defeat in a battle to the west of Caersws, described in detail by Tacitus the great Roman historian, brought his eight years of struggle to an end.

His wife and daughter were taken prisoner but Caradog succeeded in escaping to the court of Cartimandua, queen of the Brigantes in northern England. By what appears to have been an act of betrayal she put him in the hands of the Romans. Tacitus tells the story as part of the history of the conquest of Britain.

Caradog and his family were taken to Rome as prisoners, and there he was marched in irons through the city streets in a victory parade. His noble and courageous demeanour created a deep impression. Tacitus quotes his words before the emperor:

> Ambitious Rome aims at conquering the world; does the whole human race therefore have to bend to the yoke? For years I resisted successfully: I am now in your hands. If vengeance be your intention, proceed: the scene of bloodshed will soon be over, and Caradog's name will fall into oblivion. If you spare my life, I shall be an eternal memorial to the mercy of Rome.

The name of this first Welsh historical hero was long remembered in Wales. For centuries the name Caradog appears in the royal houses of the land of the Silurians.

The resistance of the Welsh was far from ending with the capture of Caradog. Indeed, in the following year a legion was defeated by the Silurians. Five years later the emperor Nero had to command that the whole of the island be brought under Roman control. Dr John Davies says that for centuries one-tenth of the Roman legions was stationed in Britain, although the area of the province was less than one-thirtieth of that of the territories of Rome. Roman losses were so heavy that withdrawal from the island was considered. Although they succeeded in destroying the druids when they attacked Ynys Môn (Anglesey), yet as late as AD 79, a generation after the initial invasion, Roman forces amounting to thirty thousand men were engaged in the north and west. It is significant that, of the three legions in Britain, two were long stationed in Caerleon and Chester and that there were at least thirty-five auxiliary camps in and near Wales.

Germanising Britain Begins

Some of the legionaries were Germanic even in the early years of the Roman invasion and their numbers steadily increased. These tended to stay in Britain permanently. By about AD 300 a considerable Germanic-Roman culture had developed in eastern Britain. A century and a half later German communities in the Thames Valley began to establish small kingdoms. Hengist and Horsa were probably invited by Gwrtheyrn (Vortigern) to help him resist a Pictish invasion in the middle of the fifth century, but Bede's assertion that there was a massive Germanic invasion was wholly mistaken, although there were large English settlements in eastern England.

It was centuries later, after the Danish conquest of the collection of Germanic kingdoms, that England and an English nation emerged. Even Harold, king of England, killed in the battle of Hastings, was a Viking descended from the Viking conquerors of the Germanic kingdoms. Hereward the Wake, best known of the resisters to William the Conqueror, was a Dane.

A Germanic victory near Bath in the sixth century cut Wales off from the Welsh-speaking south-west. Somerset came into the possession of the Germans in the seventh century, Devon in the eighth and Cornwall in the tenth century.

The Welsh Kingdoms of the Old North

There were still four Welsh-language kingdoms in the seventh century in northern England and southern Scotland, known in Welsh as Yr Hen Ogledd (The Old North). They were Ystrad Clud (Strathclyde), its capital at Dumbarton above Glasgow; Rheged, which included Cumbria, its capital at Caerliwelydd (Carlisle); Gododdin, centred on Edinburgh. The court poets at Rheged and Gododdin were Taliesin and Aneirin, the fathers of Welsh poetry, who sang of the heroic defence of their lands. The fourth Welsh kingdom was Elfed, the only one wholly in England, its centre in or near Leeds. There was warfare for two generations between the Welsh kingdoms and Northumberland, the biggest of all Germanic kingdoms at that time. The first to fall was Elfed, then Gododdin was conquered before the middle of the seventh century and Rheged before its end, nearly three centuries after the final departure of the Romans. Ystrad Clud remained independent for another three centuries before being absorbed by Scotland through marriage.

In the conquered kingdoms the Welsh language was obliterated with time and all sense of Welsh nationhood was expunged.

Cymru (Wales) is Born

The story of the liberation of the people of the land that would become Cymru (Wales) is an extraordinary one. It involved a Roman emperor who was born and bred in Celtic Galicia. Before he left the shores of Britain in AD 383 with a battle standard bearing a dragon at the head of his troops, after being proclaimed Roman emperor by his troops, Magnus Maximus transferred responsibility for the defence and government of Wales to leading families in the infrastructure created during the Roman occupation. These families became royal houses which ruled the canton-sized states. It was the implementation of this policy by Magnus Maximus that made it possible for Professor Gwyn Alf Williams to say, 'Wales is born in AD 383 with Macsen Wledig'. Magnus Maximus made a deep impact on Welsh life and legend. At least three royal houses claimed descent from him and one of the most entertaining Mabinogion stories is entitled *Breuddwyd Macsen Wledig* (The Dream of Macsen Wledig).

Irish colonists had been allowed to settle in Wales during the later years of the Roman occupation, particularly in the south and north

Magnus Maximus

13

west, but according to Nennius who wrote about AD 800 they came in great numbers after the departure of the Romans. In consequence Brittonic-speaking Cunedda came with his eight sons from near Stirling in Scotland to expel them from the northern part of Wales. In this way a Celt from Scotland ensured that Wales would be a Welsh-speaking, not an Irish-speaking, land. According to tradition Cunedda founded the royal line which would rule Gwynedd for seven centuries.

A Celtic Confraternity

A couple of generations later relations between Wales and Ireland became more friendly. A rich Celtic civilisation developed around the Irish Sea. The western seaways had become vitally important in the centuries following the barbarian conquest of the western Roman empire. They united the Celtic lands from the Old North in Scotland, Ireland, the Isle of Man, Wales, Cornwall to Brittany which had been colonised from the south-west of Britain and Wales in the sixth century.

The Celtic Church fostered relations between Wales and Ireland and Brittany in particular. The Irish scholar P.A.Wilson says that, 'All the great names of the first century of the age of saints in the Irish church … were British-trained, either directly or at one remove, or in the case of St Columbus at two removes.' He adds that, 'Wales, and particularly western and southern Wales, was the epicentre of that great missionary effort which spread by the western sea-routes to Iceland and to Spain, and which we think of as Celtic Christianity.' It is not insignificant that

St Patrick was a Briton who was a member of the third generation of a Christian family perhaps in the Severn Valley.

The relations between English and Welsh Christians were more unhappy. When the Pope sent a mission of forty or more clerics in 597, two centuries after the birth of Patrick, to convert the pagan English, the Celtic Church in Wales was asked to send a deputation to discuss the project with St Augustine, their leader. The history is written by Bede, the anti-Welsh Northumbrian scholar. There were two meetings, the first of which was held somewhere half way between Wales and Canterbury. The Welsh discovered that besides helping to convert the English they were being asked to lay aside the distinctive marks of the Celtic Church and to obey Augustine as the Archbishop of Canterbury. The Britons, says Bede, 'could not give up their customs without getting their people's consent'.

According to Bede, seven British bishops attended the second fateful meeting, some of them perhaps from Cornwall and the Old North. Bede also says that they were accompanied by a number of learned men from the great monastery at Bangor Iscoed. Before the conference the deputation consulted a wise hermit and took his advice. 'If he is a man of God,' said the hermit, referring to Augustine, 'follow him.' But how were they to know whether or not he was a man of God? The hermit's answer to this question was a quotation from the Gospel according to Saint Matthew – and remember that this is in Bede's report. 'Shoulder my yoke and learn from me, for I am gentle and humble in heart.' If he were gentle and humble, Augustine should be followed; if he were proud and severe, Christian truth was not in him and his leadership should not be accepted; he should not be recognized as their archbishop. How to judge? 'Arrange that he and his companions arrive first,' said the hermit. 'If he gets on his feet when you come to him, listen humbly to him, for he is the servant of God; but if he scorns you by remaining seated and not rising when you arrive, then you must treat him with contempt.' Augustine did not rise to greet them, and so the Britons did not accept him as their archbishop and they rejected his demands.

Augustine, says Bede, was extremely agitated by the British attitude and made dour threats. If they did not do what he asked, according to Bede's report, they would have to face war from their enemies. If they refused to cooperate with him in evangelising the English, the British would suffer the vengeance of death at their hands.

And indeed that is what happened. Aethelfrith, the pagan king of Northumbria, attacked Powys and defeated and killed its king Selyf in the battle of Chester, 616, and, again according to Bede, slaughtered 1200 Welsh monks of the monastery of Bangor Is-coed, the pearl of Cymric religious and intellectual life. The immediate reason for the slaughter, said Bede, who approved the massacre, was that the monks had prayed for Welsh success in the battle.

Cymru is a Nation, Christian and Cultured

Wales was a nation more than a thousand years before Great Britain came into existence. It emerged from a thousand years of Celtic civilization in Ynys Prydain (The Isle of Britain). Although it did not have a single state to unite it, it was distinguished from the Teuton peoples to the east by territory, language, law, customs, traditions, history and religion. The names of hundreds of saints from the fourth to the seventh centuries still ring like bells throughout the land. It was in the sixth century that the Welshman began to call himself a *Cymro* (fellow-countryman), plural – *Cymry*; the land of Wales – *Cymru*. 'Welsh', the word used by the Teutons, means a foreigner who has been under Roman rule. The Welsh language (*Cymraeg*) developed from Brittonic during the centuries which saw the Christianising of Wales, the fourth to the early seventh centuries. Welsh literature began its glorious history in the sixth century. The fathers of Welsh literature sang in the early Welsh of the Old North, Taliesin in Caerliwelydd (Carlisle) and Aneirin in Caeredin (Edinburgh). For a thousand years Welsh literature would be one of the great literatures of Europe, in prose as well as poetry, in quantity and in quality.

Taliesin and Aneirin, who were very conscious of the Britons as the native people of the Isle of Britain, sang of their heroic defence of their land and freedom. Their poems contained striking passages, vivid battle scenes and a linguistic vigour which is difficult to convey in translation. A stanza from Owain's 'Death-Song' will serve to illustrate Taliesin's quality:

Cysgid Loegr llydan nifer
    A lleufer yn eu llygaid,
A rhai ni ffoynt haeach
    A oeddynt hyach na rhaid.

Sleepeth the wide host of England
    With light in their eyes,
And those that had not fled
    Were braver than were wise.

Aneirin's greatest classic is the *Gododdin* which, as Professor Jarman says, celebrates the matchless bravery and the unswerving loyalty of the war-band of three hundred who fought against overwhelming odds until they met their end in battle, deeming retreat before a superior enemy unthinkable and choosing death before shame. They were feasted by the king of Gododdin for a year before all but the poet himself were killed in the battle of Catraeth (Catterick).

Gwŷr a aeth Gatraeth oedd ffraeth eu llu,
Glasfedd eu hancwyn, a gwenwyn fu;
Trichant trwy beiriant yn catáu
Ac wedi elwch tawelwch fu.

The men who went to Catraeth were a speedy band
Fresh mead their feast, it became poison;
Three hundred were in order embattled,
And after rejoicing there came silence.

Arthur Halts the Germanic Advance

After the collapse of Roman authority the biggest figure in Ynys Prydain, the Isle of Britain, as the Welsh called it, was Gwrtheyrn (Vortigern) whose reign seems to have included the third, fourth and fifth decades of the fifth century. He became exceedingly unpopular for introducing German auxiliaries to strengthen the defence against the Picts, although this had been Roman policy for three centuries. The Roman legions had included German soldiers who settled in Britain at the end of their military term. When the Romans left Britain there were already considerable Romano-German settlements in the cities and the countryside. Some of these organised little kingdoms in areas like Kent and the Thames Valley, sometimes assisted by Germans who had been driven out of northern Gaul by the Franks.

But the German advance was slow, far slower than the barbarian advances anywhere else in Europe. There was never any one great invasion of Angles, Saxons and Jutes as Bede had insisted. A hundred years later the greater part of present-day England was controlled by the Britons, speaking a Brittonic language.

But the situation was fatally changed by the terrible Yellow Plague which, spreading from the continent, is thought to have been at least as disastrous as the Black Death. But while the Germanic people seem to have escaped its worst consequences, it had a catastrophic effect on the Britons and their struggle for freedom. It may have exterminated the majority of the Welsh-speaking people who ruled western Britain.

The most interesting and most mysterious man to lead the

defence of the Britons against the English was Arthur, who was probably an independent military commander of cavalry similar to those found among the Roman armed forces. This great Welsh hero was subsequently appropriated by the English. Of the twelve victories attributed to him by Nennius in the early ninth century, the one most widely accepted was at Mount Badon near Bath, fought in 516 according to the *Annales Cambriae*, but probably a decade or two earlier. This vitally important battle confined the barbarians to a few areas, including Kent and the Thames Valley, and secured fifty years of peace.

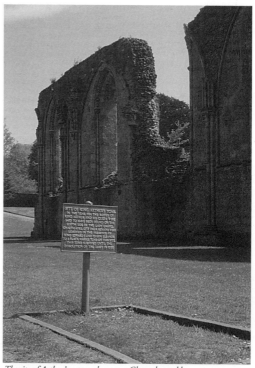

The site of Arthur's supposed grave at Glastonbury abbey

Heirs to Romano-British Civilisation

The development of the Welsh language from Brittonic, and of Welsh culture, coincided with the Christian revolution. In religion and culture the Cymry were heirs to Romano-British civilisation, and the Welsh language contains over a thousand Latin words, many of them for simple things for which there must have been Brittonic equivalents. G.M.Trevelyan goes as far as to say that, 'The Welsh of the fifth and sixth centuries came to regard their Christianity as their distinguishing mark which, together with their love of bardic music and poetry, enabled them to feel superior to the Saxon savages.' The Celtic Church retained its independence in Wales until the late eighth century, three-quarters of a century longer than in Scotland and nearly a century and a half longer than in Ireland.

Its most prominent Christian leader was Dewi Sant (St David), Wales's patron saint, who lived in the sixth century in the middle period of the great Christian surge. He raised his monastery at St David's near a port on the Pembrokeshire coast, in an area which had been peacefully settled by Irish colonisers in the third century to the enrichment of Welsh life and literature. St David himself almost certainly spoke Irish as well as Welsh. In his day St David's was a bustling seaport, a veritable Crewe Junction of the seaways, said Gwyn Alf Williams. Many Irish monks and scholars came to stay at the monastery.

The Church's main intellectual centre was the great monastery at Llantwit Major (Llanilltud Fawr) near the Vale of Glamorgan coast, where the abbot in the late fifth century and early sixth century was Illtud, the greatest Celtic scholar of the age.

Many famous political and religious leaders, including a number of the most prominent Christian leaders of Brittany, were educated there.

The most powerful political leader to be educated at the feet of Illtud was Maelgwn Gwynedd, king of Gwynedd and British over-king. A contemporary student of Maelgwn's was Gildas, a native of Strathclyde who became a strong influence in Ireland and Brittany but who is best known as the author of a provocative book, *Concerning the Fall of Britain*, written in Latin during the half a century of peace secured by Arthur's great victory in the battle of Mons Badonicus. Maelgwn Gwynedd, himself an able military and political leader, lived in this period and died in 549 of the terrible Yellow Plague which had little effect on the Germanic people but devastated the Britons, mortally weakening their power of resistance.

The Yellow Plague must have made possible the virtually unopposed advance of Mercia towards Powys and the conquest of Elfed by Edwin, king of Northumbria. Edwin even attacked Ynys Môn (Anglesey), but was thrown back by its king Cadwallon. Then, perhaps hoping to prevent further Northumbrian aggression, Cadwallon, in alliance with Penda, king of Mercia, attacked Northumberland, defeated its army and killed Edwin. In the following year Cadwallon defeated and killed Edwin's successors. But in the next year, in a battle near Hadrian's Wall, Cadwallon himself was defeated and killed. His death ended the last possibility of restoring British hegemony in the Isle of Britain. Three centuries had passed since the fall of the Empire. The Germanic peoples had taken a far longer time to overcome resistance in Britain than in the other countries of western Europe.

Some of today's England remained in the possession of the Britons until the end of the eighth century. Devon still had a British king in the year 710 and Cornwall was not absorbed by Wessex until the middle of the tenth century.

In the south-west a defeat of the Britons in the battle of Dyrham near Bristol in 577 drew Wessex to the Severn's southern bank and separated the Welsh of Wales from their fellow Britons in Somerset, Devon and Cornwall. However, the powerful resistance of the men of Gwent and their notable victory in the middle of the seventh century ensured that Gwent and Glamorgan remained Welsh.

The struggle for Powys, which had included most of Shropshire and Cheshire, and whose capital had been in or near Shrewsbury, was bitterly destructive. It was the subject of some of the most deeply moving poems in the Welsh language. Whereas heroism dominated the poetry of the Old North, anguished heartbreak characterised the ninth-century poetry of Powys. In one cycle of the poems, prince Llywarch Hen (The Old) calls into question in his decrepit old age the martial ideal which had governed his life as a warrior. Facing his inevitable fate he identifies himself with a fallen leaf:

> Y ddeilen hon neus cynired gwynt –
>> Gwae hi o'i thynged!
> Hi hen; eleni ganed.

> *The wind carries away this leaf –*
>> *alas for its fate!*
> *It's old, though born only this year.*

In another cycle of a hundred and thirteen short verses, princess Heledd mourns the loss of her much-loved brothers, especially Cynddylan, who had all been killed in battle defending Pengwern near Shrewsbury, the site of the Powys court.

> Ystafell Cynddylan ys tywyll heno
> Heb dân, heb wely.
> Wylaf wers, tawaf wedy.
>
> *Dark is Cynddylan's hall tonight*
> *With no fire, no bed.*
> *I weep awhile, then am silent.*

With the westward expansion of Mercia and the early seventh century wars against Powys, the final demarcation of the land frontier of the Wales we know was almost complete. It was marked in the eighth century by the imposing Dyke built by Offa, king of Mercia. Offa consulted the kings of Powys and Gwent whilst constructing the Dyke, for its purpose was not defensive as in Hadrian's Wall but to denote the frontier clearly. Forty kilometres at the northern end were not completed, probably because Offa was killed in the battle of Rhuddlan in 796. F.M. Stanton describes Offa's Dyke as 'the outstanding memorial of its type and period in north western Europe'. It is a tribute to the remarkable tenacity of the Welsh that parts of the land on the Mercian side of the Dyke are now in Wales.

Reinvigoration of Welsh Life

Wales was in a difficult, even dangerous, position at the end of the eighth and the beginning of the ninth century. As English power grew, English attacks on Welsh kingdoms north and south became more frequent, some threatening permanent occupation. Fortunately, a strong and cultured man, Merfyn Frych, a descendant of Cunedda, became king of Gwynedd. He not only ensured the survival of the kingdom but stimulated an intellectual revival. His descent from the princes of the Old North stirred an interest in the literature and history of the northern Welsh kingdoms. His court became a staging post for Irish scholars on their way to the court of Charlemagne and his son. Perhaps this was the time of the transfer of the poems of Taliesin and Aneirin from the Old North, possibly from Strathclyde which was still Welsh-speaking and would remain so for a few centuries. It was the time when Nennius wrote the *Historia Brittonum* which purports to convey the history of the Britons from Julius Caesar to the seventh century. Although Nennius is far from dependable, his is the source of most of our knowledge of the relations of Magnus Maximus with Britain, of Cunedda, Vortigern, Germanus, Ambrosius and especially Arthur. This interest in history was far from being confined to the court of Merfyn Frych, 'the magnificent king of the Britons'. Nora Chadwick, an authority on this period, wrote, 'Round about the beginning of the ninth century there seems to have been a heightened intellectual activity and a keen sense of nationalism throughout all the Celtic countries.'

Nor was this intellectual vigour confined to the Celtic

countries. It was indicated by Alfred the Great's request to Asser of St David's to help him to civilise Wessex. It is from Asser's *Life of Alfred* that we learn how Alfred burnt the cakes. The Gwynedd court continued to be cultured when Merfyn's son Rhodri inherited the throne. When Rhodri inherited Powys through his mother, and a southern kingdom through his brother, his government extended from Anglesey to Gower. He made his name as a military leader. He became known as Rhodri Mawr (the Great) for contending so effectively with the ravages of the English and the Vikings, known in Wales as the Black Pagans. The latter lay waste great parts of the continent, and when Alfred the Great ascended the Wessex throne the whole of England, except for southern Wessex, was under Danish control. Rhodri's notable victory in which the Danish leader Horm was killed was celebrated in the Frankish court, in a poem by the Irish poet and scholar Sedulius Scottus.

It was not against the Black Pagans, however, that Rhodri met his end. His thirty-four years' rule ended in 877 when he and his son Gwriad were killed in battle against the English. Welsh confidence remained high even after this grave loss. Three years later they heavily defeated the English in a battle near Conwy which they said was 'God's revenge for the killing of Rhodri'. The major kings and princes until the Norman Conquest could claim to be descendants of Rhodri the Great, and by peacefully uniting most of Wales under his rule he established a theme which was to run through Welsh history for more than four hundred years.

Codification of Welsh Law in the Welsh Language

Despite a long succession of attacks by the English, and even more by the Danes, Anarawd, who succeeded his father Rhodri the Great, kept the kingdom of Gwynedd and Powys intact during his important long thirty-eight year reign. He was succeeded by Hywel, a grandson of Rhodri. Hywel was one of the most notable of Welsh kings, not only because he created the kingdom of Deheubarth (the Southern Part) and peacefully gathered the whole of Wales, excepting the south-east, under his government, and not only because he became known as Hywel Dda (the Good), but mainly because he was responsible, over a thousand years ago, for giving cohesion to Welsh laws by codifying them. Welsh law, which became known as *Cyfraith Hywel* (the Law of Hywel), was of an impressively high

The Law Book of Hywel Dda

standard. It contained, as Professor Dafydd Jenkins has shown, elements of respect for women and children, mercy and common sense, which have only recently been incorporated into English law. Furthermore, *Cyfraith Hywel* was a Welsh-language classic which illustrated the ability of the language to express the most subtle nuances of the law at a time when, throughout Europe, Latin was the language of the law. Joseph Loth's opinion was that 'From an intellectual point of view it is the laws which give the Welsh the greatest claim to fame.' One of its most profound effects was to deepen the sense of nationhood. From Ynys Môn to Gwent, the law was *Cyfraith Hywel.*

Hywel may have been inspired by the law of Rome, which he visited when at the height of his powers, and also by his admiration for Alfred the Great. Although Hywel was the high king of Wales he acknowledged what Trevelyan called 'the vague supremacy' of revived Wessex which was on its way to a conquest – albeit a temporary one – of the Danes. This was the only realistic policy open to him. Nevertheless, it disgusted some Welshmen whose aversion was voiced dramatically in *Armes Prydein,* the greatest prophetic poem in the Welsh language. Written about the year 930, the poem called on the Welsh to unite with the men of the Old North, the Irish, the Cornishmen and the Bretons to restore England to British rule. A memory of past Brythonic rule still lingered to reinforce the hatred of the arrogance of Athelstan of Wessex. The men of Scotland, Strathclyde and Dublin did unite but were defeated by Athelstan in the battle of Brunanburh in 937.

Black Pagans and Golden Literature

The kingdom of Deheubarth was inherited on Hywel's death by his son Owain, who during his thirty-eight year reign commissioned the compilation of the genealogies and the *Annales Cambriae* which are essential to the understanding of Welsh history from the sixth to the tenth centuries. Owain was succeeded by Hywel's grandson Maredudd, 'the most illustrious king of the Welsh', who restored the united kingdom of his grandfather and ruled the land from Ynys Môn to Pembroke in a reign which lasted until 999. Internal violence was far from being absent, but Hywel's dynasty gave Wales a century of comparative stability. This contrasted with the condition of its English neighbour. 'War, invasion and bloodshed,' says Trevelyan, 'were the normal conditions of life in Saxon England.'

At the end of the tenth century the ravages of the Black Pagans were at their most destructive. Although they did not conquer Wales or occupy any large part of it they devastated Welsh coastal areas and demolished or plundered many great monasteries including Llantwit Major, Llancarfan, Llanbadarn, St Dogmael's and St David's, where they killed the bishop. They conquered England and occupied great areas. Eventually Canute made England the centre of his Viking empire.

Despite the violence there was much splendid literature in poetry and prose and considerable fine scholarship. The nature poems of the period were especially delightful. A poem of the early tenth century in praise of Tenby is particularly attractive. 'Addwyn gaer y sydd ar glawr gweilgi' (There is a gentle fort on the ocean dyke). Composed in the beautiful Welsh spoken at that time in the south of Pembrokeshire, it describes the cheerful life of the fort.

But the glory of the prose literature of the Middle Ages is in the magnificent stories known as the *Mabinogion*. Great prose literature in an indigenous language is very rare indeed in Europe in the Middle Ages as Latin alone was considered sufficiently dignified for legal or literary work. But as Sir Thomas Parry wrote of the *Mabinogion*, 'It is almost impossible to over-emphasise the literary power of the man who gave their final shape to the *Pedair Cainc* (Four Branches). It is in the power of expression that his greatness lies. He has the first essential of a writer – in that he is a master of his medium, that is to say, the language. He knows all its idioms, and he writes in harmony with its purest qualities...' Ernest Renan, the great Breton scholar, wrote of the influence of the stories:

> 'It was through the *Mabinogion* that the Welsh imagination influenced the Continent; it transformed in the twelfth century the poetic art of Europe and realised this miracle, that the creation of a small nation which had been forgotten had become a feast of imagination for mankind over all the earth... Above all else, by creating woman's character the Welsh romances caused one of the greatest revolutions known to literary historians. It was like an electric spark; in a few years the taste of Europe was transformed.'

Just as *Cyfraith Hywel* was a Welsh literary classic, so too *The Chronicle of the Princes* (*Brut y Tywysogion*), probably composed in Strata Florida, was written with such mastery that it can be considered a part of Welsh literature. Of course the *Brut* was not widely known. It was a historical tract studied by scholars and probably unknown to the Welsh professional story-tellers *(cyfarwyddiaid)* who delighted people in many countries with tales which, says Gwyn Alf Williams, were 'a brilliant and breath-taking world of myth, legend, half-history, folk-tale, and sheer, marvellous invention...'

A United Wales

The *Mabinogion* were written during the reign of Gruffudd ap Llywelyn, the only king to rule over the whole of Wales. The success of this able warrior king was attained through violence. He even invaded England, the first Welsh ruler to do so since Cadwallon in the seventh century, and won back territories that had been in English hands for centuries, including Radnor and Presteigne, Chirk and Bangor Is-coed, Whitford and Hope. Harold, then earl of Wessex, attacked him by land and sea and forced Gruffudd to fly for refuge to the mountains of Snowdonia, where he was killed by a Welshman who was probably avenging the death of his father. Three years later Harold himself was killed in the battle of Hastings. Gruffudd ap Llywelyn founded no dynasty but, says J.E. Lloyd, 'He bequeathed to the Welsh people the priceless legacy of a revived national spirit.' That is more than can be said for Harold. King Harold married Gruffudd ap Llywelyn's widow, Lady Godiva's grand-daughter. It is not reported that she protested against the humiliation of becoming queen of England after the glory of being queen of Wales.

The Norman Invasion

If the period of the fifth to the seventh century is considered to be the first Welsh heroic age, the eleventh to the thirteenth century can be regarded as the second. For whereas England was conquered by the Normans in weeks, it took centuries for the Normans with the might of the Anglo-Norman empire behind them to overcome the resistance of the Welsh. A generation after being ruled by Canute the Viking conqueror, William the Norman – conqueror of England – replaced Anglo Saxon with French as the language of law and government and in cultural life, whereas in Wales Welsh continued to be the language of law and government for another two and a quarter centuries and is still the language of the cultural life of a substantial part of the population. In England the Normans despised the native aristocracy, but in Wales they treated the Welsh aristocracy as equals.

Soon after the battle of Hastings, William the Conqueror established three powerful earldoms on the border of Wales, at Chester, Shrewsbury and Hereford. These were the first of the self-governing military entities to compose the March which for centuries played such an important part in the life of Wales. The Marcher Lords had exceptional powers, including the right to their own courts and independent law, and to build castles and employ armies. Unlike the English shires, the Marcher Lordships were powerful independent entities not responsible to English government, though the Lords Marcher were subjects of the English king.

The two outstanding Welsh leaders to face Norman power at the end of the decade following the battle of Hastings were Rhys ap Tewdwr and Gruffudd ap Cynan. Rhys, who was descended from Hywel Dda and Rhodri Mawr, was the king of the southern kingdom of Deheubarth. William the Conqueror made an agreement with him when he came to St David's in 1081. Although there was an element of vassalage in it, peaceful relations with the Norman barons were secured for a dozen years.

Gruffudd ap Cynan was less fortunate during those years. His background was unusual. He was born and bred in Ireland where his father, a descendant of Rhodri Mawr, lived in exile. His mother was the daughter of the Norse king of Dublin, so that Gruffudd was half Viking. During the turbulent early years after claiming his inheritance, he had to flee for refuge back to Ireland four times. During those years the Normans established their headquarters in Degannwy and built castles as far west as Ynys Môn and Merioneth.

The first Norman attacks on Welsh land were made in Gwent, where they built castles as the Romans had built forts, in Chepstow, Monmouth, Caerleon, Wigmore, Clifford and Ewyas Harold. The earliest were motte and bailey castles, of which they built five hundred in Wales. Although the ancient kingdom of Gwent was demolished by them the uplands remained in Welsh hands, as they did in Glamorgan, and the Welsh language remained the tongue of the people until the nineteenth century when industrial Gwent produced the greatest Welsh-language poet of the century in the person of Islwyn. Small towns grew around the stone castles. It was in Gwent that the first of eighty English-speaking castle towns were built. Of course, they added considerably to the effect of the castles and other anglicising influences.

Most of the kingdom of Powys had fallen into Norman hands and while Gruffudd ap Cynan was a refugee in Ireland the powerful Robert of Rhuddlan had been recognised by William the Conqueror as lord of Gwynedd, with his court at Degannwy, where Maelgwn Gwynedd had held court five centuries earlier. The Welsh situation became still more desperate when Gruffudd ap Cynan was captured by Robert, languishing in prison for twelve years. Despite Robert's death in battle against the Welsh, the Normans succeeded in penetrating still more deeply into western Gwynedd.

Normans on the Rampage

The southern situation was transformed in 1093 when Rhys ap Tewdwr, the last to be called King of Deheubarth, was killed in battle near Brecon whilst defending his kingdom. His death destroyed the Welsh defensive bulwark. It 'opened the floodgates of Norman rapacity,' said Sir J.E. Lloyd, 'and its trickling rills now united in one great deluge that swept the country from end to end'. Southern Wales was overwhelmed; the lowlands of Glamorgan fell into Norman hands, and castles were built at strong points on the western coast, including Cardigan and Pembroke. The only remnant of the kingdom of Deheubarth left to Rhys ap Tewdwr's son Gruffydd was the commote of Caeo. He was a king without a kingdom.

Thus, a generation after the battle of Hastings, the whole of Wales – north and south – appeared to be subdued. Even the great power of the Norman French Church was used ruthlessly to subjugate the Welsh; the character of the Welsh Church was destroyed. It was in this period that a strong plantation of Flemings was established in the south of Pembrokeshire, displacing the Welsh language permanently.

But the Welsh fought on with guerrilla tactics, harrying the Normans ceaselessly. There were few set battles. Within a few years of the death of Rhys ap Tewdwr they could claim remarkable successes both in the north and the south.

The Cymry Fight Back

In the north, Gruffudd ap Cynan escaped from prison to lead the struggle. By the end of the eleventh century every Norman castle to the west of Conwy was in Welsh hands. The whole of Gwynedd was cleared. King John led a combined land and sea attack which made little impression, but a powerful invasion led by the earl of Chester forced Gruffudd to retreat to Ynys Môn and then once more to seek refuge in Ireland. However the men of Powys, under Cadwgan son of Bleddyn, attacked districts in Shropshire and Cheshire and even seized the key castle of Montgomery.

The men of the south displayed similar resolution. Excepting only Pembroke and Rhyd-y-gors near Carmarthen, all the Norman castles of Dyfed and Ceredigion were destroyed. When king William Rufus had to invade to try to save his feudal deputies, and penetrated deeply into northern territory, he was forced to retreat. The men of Brycheiniog (Breconshire) and Gwent also rose. Although they did not capture castles they defeated Norman armies at Ystradgynlais and the Gower, and in Gwent itself. Pembroke castle, under Gerald of Windsor, was the strong base from which the Normans counter-attacked, aided by a more successful invasion by king William Rufus. Yet Ceredigion and Ystrad Tywi still remained in Welsh hands.

During Gruffudd ap Cynan's forced withdrawal to Ireland there occurred one of the most dramatic events in Welsh history. The great navy of Magnus Barefoot, king of Norway, anchored off the coast of Ynys Môn. The Vikings landed, met the Normans in battle and trounced them so heavily that they never tried to colonise Anglesey again.

Gruffudd made his fourth return from Ireland. This time, with extraordinary tenacity, he built a powerful kingdom which he ruled for a further thirty-eight years. Although Gwynedd endured another royal invasion, the growth of the state's power made it the acknowledged leader of the Welsh nation. When William Rufus died, although the Norman lordships remained, by far the greater part of Wales was under Welsh government.

The difficulties of Cadwgan, prince of Powys, were augmented by his son Owain, who fell in love with the beautiful Nest, the wife of Gerald of Windsor, leader of the Normans in Dyfed and Castellan of Pembroke castle. Nest had been given in marriage to Gerald after the death of her father Rhys ap Tewdwr, the last king of Deheubarth, an early example of Norman-Welsh inter-marriage that became so common. Apart from her children by Gerald, she had children by three other Normans including Henry I, king of England. Three sons of hers became bishops; one was the bishop of St David's for twenty-eight years. Three further sons, the FitzStephens and the FitzGeralds, led the first conquerors of Ireland, and the FitzGeralds especially played a prominent part in Irish life, becoming more Irish than the Irish. Nest's daughter Angharad was the mother of Giraldus Cambrensis whom we will meet again as the man who fought long and courageously to convert St David's into a Welsh archbishopric independent of Canterbury.

But it was with Owain of Powys that Nest eloped, challenging the king as well as Gerald her husband. This led to a powerful attack on Ceredigion, which was ruled by the house of Powys. Owain fled to Ireland, and a few years later paid for his rashness with his life, but not before forcing Henry I to occupy Ceredigion himself.

Freedom is Established

By this time Norman power extended over virtually the whole of the fertile lowlands of southern Wales. English peasants laboured in the Englishries around the castles and castle towns. But in the Welshries of the hills the traditional Cymric way of life persisted. It was from the afforested hilly commote of Caeo that Gruffydd, the son of king Rhys ap Tewdwr, challenged Norman rule after returning from Ireland, where he had taken refuge after his father was killed. Gathering young men behind him, he fought a guerrilla war to regain his heritage. His country's youth were enthused by his series of modest successes such as the destruction of Narberth castle and partial destruction of Swansea and Llandovery castles and his threat to the safety of the royal town of Carmarthen. As his power grew he reduced the castles of Blaen

Porth and Peithyll and even attacked Ceredigion.

Gruffudd ap Rhys's wife was Gwenllïan, daughter of Gruffudd ap Cynan of Gwynedd, who had amazingly withstood the simultaneous invasion of three royal armies which came from three directions to converge at Trawsfynydd. The southern army included men from Devon and Cornwall; Henry I led the second army from the south-east over the Berwyn Mountains; the third, which assembled at Chester, was led by Alexander I of Scotland. This great array of power achieved little. After over half a century of strenuous struggle, Gruffudd ap Cynan was secure for the rest of his long life, free to enjoy the music and literature in which he delighted. He was the only Welsh king or prince to be the subject of a contemporary biography.

Princess Gwenllïan Killed in Battle

The death of Henry I on 1 December 1135 gave new impetus to the struggle of the Welsh, who threw themselves against the Normans in a great surge of energy. On New Year's Day 1136 Hywel ap Maredudd of Brycheiniog (Breconshire), which included the upper part of the Swansea Valley, led his men against the large Anglo-Norman settlement in Gower and in a battle near the Llwchwr river won a stunning victory in which five hundred of the enemy were said to have been killed. Immediately on receipt of the astonishing news, Gruffudd ap Rhys made for Gwynedd to seek the help of Gruffudd ap Cynan, his father-in-law, and of his son Owain, to expel the Normans from Ceredigion.

When Gruffudd ap Rhys was away, his wife Gwenllïan felt

impelled to lead an army against the powerful Norman military strongpoint at Cydweli (Kidwelly). She led her army, said Giraldus Cambrensis a generation later, 'like a queen of the Amazons and a second Pentesilea', showing the spirit which immortalised her. Both she and her son Morgan were killed in a battle near the mighty Cydweli castle on land still known

A memorial stone to Gwenllïan, near Cydweli castle, erected in the early 1990s

as Maes Gwenllïan. So did the daughter of a king and the wife of a prince who was the son of a king, give her life for her land and its freedom. Her son Rhys, who would be the saviour of Cymru's southern half, was four years of age at the time.

Gwenllïan's death was avenged a few months later by a tremendous Welsh victory at Cardigan after Owain and Cadwaladr, sons of Gruffudd ap Cynan, had marched through Ceredigion with an army which now included a large cavalry contingent, capturing a number of castles on the way. They were joined by Gruffudd ap Rhys and two Powys princes. Near Cardigan a powerful Anglo-Norman army gathered from every part of the south to defend the most important Norman centre in Ceredigion. Their fate was to be hurled headlong into the town and over the Teifi estuary bridge, which collapsed under their weight throwing hundreds to a watery death. Following this calamity king Stephen led an army into Wales to restore Norman rule in Ceredigion, but failed to get beyond Brecon. Gruffudd ap Rhys successfully attacked Dyfed, but then he died in the prime of life, to be remembered as one who, without despairing in the darkest times, kept the flame of freedom burning.

Owain Gwynedd and Cadwaladr completed the reconquest of Ceredigion by taking castles as far as Llansteffan and North Pembroke. They even captured Carmarthen castle and town, the royal centre of south-west Wales. Welsh government was also restored in Cantref Bychan, centred on Llandovery, and in the mid-Wales principality of Maeliennydd, while Morgan ab Owain occupied Usk castle and established himself there as the Lord of Caerleon. Although the national resurgence transformed the political situation, the Norman Marcher Lordships remained powerful. Carmarthen was recovered for the government. Yet all the enormous power of England and the Norman empire could not quench the spirit of the Welsh.

The Rule of the Great Princes

Although Owain Cyfeiliog, prince of Powys, was a brilliantly talented soldier, statesman and poet, the twelfth century was dominated by two of the greatest princes: Owain, prince of Gwynedd, and after him Rhys ap Gruffudd, prince of Deheubarth. Rhys was commonly known as the Lord Rhys, although his ancestors from his grandfather Rhys ap Tewdwr to Hywel Dda and Rhodri Mawr and beyond had the title 'king'. Many documents refer to him as the Prince of South Wales.

Sir J.E. Lloyd says that it was under Owain Gwynedd that the Welsh nation attained the full measure of national consciousness which enabled it for another century and a half to resist absorption into the English realm.

Prince Owain Gwynedd

After his success in restoring Welsh rule in Ceredigion, Owain Gwynedd turned his attention to the north-east where he occupied Mold Castle and built others. Madog, prince of Powys, restored Welsh rule in Oswestry for the first time since the seventh century. Madog was the patron of Cynddelw Brydydd Mawr, considered to be the greatest of court poets. The culture and political order of Wales was, however, threatened by the ascension of Henry II to the throne of England. An able, powerful and arrogant man, Henry was a bitter enemy of the Celtic countries.

Early in his reign Henry gathered a large army and navy to attack Gwynedd, but initially he was lucky to escape with his life from a well-planned attack by Owain near the north-eastern Welsh border. Many prominent Norman leaders were killed and others scattered. Nevertheless, Henry recovered sufficiently to force the Welsh to retreat to St Asaph. Meanwhile, Henry's navy had sailed with an army to Ynys Môn where they were defeated by the Welsh. Among those killed was the son of Henry I and Princess Nest. Nevertheless, Owain realised that the growth of Norman power under Henry II made necessary a rather costly agreement which compelled him to renounce the title of king. He kept most of his gains, however.

In southern Wales Rhys ap Gruffudd, the sole physically able survivor of Gwenllïan's six sons, became prince of Deheubarth at the age of twenty-three on the death of his brother Maredudd with whom he had begun his military career at thirteen years of age in a successful attack on Llansteffan castle. This was the first of a series of successes for them which culminated in the

Rhys ap Gruffudd

restoration of their government in Ceredigion. Henry II, however, reconquered most of his lands, but Rhys was not subdued for long. He was encouraged by the news of the success of the daring midnight attack on the powerful Cardiff castle, overcoming its hundred and twenty defenders and capturing the earl of Gloucester, his wife and eldest son. The author of this exploit was Rhys ap Gruffudd's brother-in-law Ifor Bach, Lord of Senghennydd which extended from Brecon to the rivers Taff and Rhymni.

Before long Rhys was again attacking Carmarthen and capturing a number of castles. When he was attacked, even on one occasion by a large force led by five earls, he would retreat to the afforested valleys of the Cantref Mawr near his fortress of Dinefwr (Dynevor). But once again Henry II led a large army against him, evoking among the Welsh, says the Chronicle, a fear that the king's intention was 'to exterminate all the Britons completely, so that the Brittanic name should never more be remembered'. Giraldus Cambrensis, however, records a more confident note struck by an old prophet in Pencader who declared to the king that 'No nation but this of the Welsh, nor any other language, will answer for this corner of the earth on the Day of terrible Judgment before the Almighty Judge.'

Rhys yielded to Henry and was taken to England. He and Owain Gwynedd and Malcolm IV, king of Scotland, paid allegiance to Henry at Woodstock. The relationship of the Scottish king with the English crown was similar to that of the Welsh princes. Rhys escaped, and returned full of explosive energy to clear the Normans once again from Ceredigion and extend his kingdom to the Dovey estuary.

Battle of the Berwyn

When Henry had been placed in a difficult position by the murder of Archbishop Becket, Owain Gwynedd challenged him by an attack led by his son on north-eastern Wales and by forging an alliance with all the Welsh princes. Henry accepted the challenge. He organised on the border of Wales a huge army, the like of which had never been seen in the countries of Britain, gathering men from every region of England and all parts of the Norman empire, from Anjou and Aquitaine and from Ireland and Scotland. The Danish navy was also hired from Ireland, and London contributed substantially to the cost. The king of England was determined to put an end to Welsh freedom for all time. By the end of July 1165 the vast array of power was ready to strike.

From every part of Wales men joined Owain's army to defend their land. Opponents cooperated; differences were sunk. Rhys ap Gruffudd and his sons left their struggle in Deheubarth; Prince Owain Cyfeiliog of Powys was there with his fellow poet prince from Gwynedd, Hywel ab Owain Gwynedd. The sons of Madog ap Maredudd were there, and so were Cadwallon and Einion Clud of the former kingdom of Wye and Severn. The national consciousness that had for centuries imbued the kingdoms and principalities of Wales was given impressive military expression. It was not Gwynedd alone but the whole of Cymru that was being defended. Cymru was united in her hour of crisis, united under one prince, Owain Gwynedd, who called himself the Prince of Wales. Thus was the truth of Giraldus Cambrensis's dictum illustrated, that if the Welsh would be inseparable they would be insuperable.

The armies of England marched from Oswestry, through Chirk and the Ceiriog Valley. There they were resisted by chosen Welsh warriors, 'and many of the strongest fell on both sides'. Then they climbed the slopes of the Berwyn Mountain and over the road still called Ffordd y Saeson (The Englishmen's Road). There the rain fell on them in torrents, bucketing incessantly while the wind screamed like a wild thing. Paths became rushing streams, camp floors were quagmires. The men were drenched by the rain, their tents torn to ribbons by the wind. As the floods increased, food decreased. As the imperial forces, blinded by the wind and the rain, laboured to advance they were harried persistently by the Welsh. The great imperial army was forced to retreat in utter humiliation. Little wonder that Henry, in a letter to the Byzantine emperor, said 'The Welsh are a people who cannot be tamed.'

Furious with anger, the king of England avenged himself brutally on his Welsh hostages, blinding or gravely injuring twenty-two of them, including two of Owain Gwynedd's sons and two of Rhys ap Gruffudd's. Churches too were burnt. Giraldus Cambrensis speaks of Owain Gwynedd's restrained response to this malign behaviour. When his young supporters told him they could never again show respect for English churches Owain said:

> I do not agree with this opinion: rather we should be grateful and joyful because of this. For we are very unequal against the English unless we are upheld by divine aid; but they, through what they have done, have made an enemy of God himself, who can avenge the injury to himself and to us at the same time.

Owain Fawr (the Great) advanced further in the north-east, destroying Dinas Basing and capturing the vitally important fortress of Rhuddlan. He also fought non-violently for the right to appoint Welsh bishops in a Church which was unscrupulously used by the Norman government as a powerful weapon to strengthen their grip on Wales. He appointed Arthur of Ynys Enlli (Bardsey Island) as bishop of Bangor. Arthur was consecrated in Ireland. Two years before his death in 1170 Owain Gwynedd sent an ambassador to the court of Louis VII in France offering aid in Louis's struggle against Henry II.

Owain had a great capacity for love. His love for his wife Cristin was so deep that he suffered excommunication rather than put her aside at the demand of the Church. He loved his children; the death of his son Rhun almost broke his heart. He loved his land to which he devoted sixty years of public service. Some of this love is also evident in the poetry of his son Hywel who wrote in a fine panegyric in the strict metres, to his homeland:

> Caraf ei morfa a'i mynyddedd,
> A'i chaer ger ei choed a'i chain diredd
> A'i dolydd a'i dwfr a'i dyffrynnedd
> A'i gwylain gwynion a'i gwymp wragedd.
> Caraf ei milwyr a'i meirch hywedd
> A'i choed a'i chedyrn a'i chyfannedd.

> *I love its coastland and its mountains,*
> *its castle near the woods and its fine lands,*
> *its water meadows and its valleys,*
> *its white gulls and its lovely women.*
> *I love its warriors, its trained stallions,*
> *its woods, its brave men and its homes.*

Rhys ap Gruffudd Restores Welsh Rule Throughout the South

Rhys ap Gruffudd, returning from the battle of the Berwyn, took the key castles of Cardigan and Cilgerran and turned the families of Clare and Clifford out of their western Marcher Lordships. After the death of Owain Gwynedd, Rhys for a generation was the greatest of the Welsh princes. The Welsh word for prince is *tywysog,* plural *tywysogion.* The literal meaning of *tywysog* is Leader. Rhys came from a family of heroic *tywysogion.* They included his brother Maredudd, his father Gruffudd ap Rhys, his mother Gwenllïan, his grandfather Rhys ap Tewdwr, king of Deheubarth, back through Hywel Dda and Rhodri Mawr. A year after Owain Gwynedd's death, Rhys's statesmanship was evinced by his reconciliation with Henry II at a meeting in the Forest of Dean. The following year saw him recognised as the Justice of the whole of southern Wales, his authority extending over Glamorgan and Gwent.

Most of the last three decades of his long rule were a time of peace and prosperity. It is true that, although the Normans had been defeated, the Marcher Lordships could still cause trouble. This was largely overcome by a stratagem adopted by Rhys which had profound, mostly unhappy, consequences in Ireland. Dermot, king of Leinster, had appealed in vain to Henry II for help in regaining his throne. He then appealed to Rhys, who saw an opportunity of ridding himself of troublesome Norman barons. He released Robert FitzStephen from prison, where he had been incarcerated since his defeat by Rhys two years previously, on condition that he led a Norman force to Ireland to help Dermot.

A part of the abbey of Ystrad Fflur (Strata Florida), where a memorial stone marks the possible spot of the grave of Wales's greatest poet, Dafydd ap Gwilym

FitzStephen was a son of the Princess Nest and, like Rhys, a grandson of king Rhys ap Tewdwr. He was joined by Maurice FitzGerald who had been lord of Llansteffan before his defeat by Rhys, and also by Raymond FitzGerald, former lord of Emlyn. Like FitzStephen, both were sons of Nest and grandsons of Rhys ap Tewdwr. Trevelyan notes that many in this last Norman conquest were sons of Welsh mothers. 'A special breed these Marcher lords,' he says, adding that 'Perhaps the Celtic elements in the blood helped their descendants to mingle only too easily with the native Irish ... But no Norman intruders in England, Sicily or Scotland ever showed themselves superior ... the chain-clad knights were supported by archers whose skill was the speciality not of England but of Wales.'

Rhys was a cultured man who rejoiced in the Welsh language (*Cymraeg*) as a national treasure and sustained it as a matter of conscious policy. The great poet Cynddelw paid tribute to him as 'Bri Brython, bugail Cymru' (The glory of the Britons, the shepherd of Wales), while for the Oxford historian A.L. Poole he was 'the man who by his unceasing efforts and fine sense of patriotism kept alive the traditions of Welsh independence and nationality'.

Rhys was at the heart of a vigorous development of Welsh civilisation in which poetry flourished, almost wholly in Welsh, though some in Latin. The bards, who were also historians, faced long and arduous training. Their poetry, with its strong appeal to the ear, was written in perhaps the most involved mannerisation of verse ever developed. Known as *cynghanedd,* it is still in common use. Prose books, particularly the lives of the saints, which flowed from the monasteries, were written mainly in Welsh, as was the great historical work *Brut y Tywysogion, The Chronicle of the Princes,* which was written mostly in Strata Florida, one of the Cistercian monasteries which influenced Welsh life and literature so profoundly. These monasteries, with an abbot at their head, were conducted on the lines of the *clas* of the Celtic Church, abolished by the Normans. They became extremely Welsh despite their continental origin. Significantly they were a papal order whose White monks were free from Canterbury control.

The position of Anglo Saxon in England was in striking contrast to the high status of the Welsh language during these centuries. After the Norman conquest the English monasteries were crowded by foreigners, says Bradley. This arrested the development of vernacular literature. Before long the boys in the monastic schools ceased to learn to read and write their native tongue and learned to read and write French, which was the language of England's law and government for centuries. A half a dozen generations after Rhys founded the Talyllychau (Talley) Abbey, the monoglot French-speaking Edward I considered it still so impossibly Welsh in character that he expelled the monks and replaced them by 'others of the English tongue'.

Some scholarly works and even poetry was written in Latin, and as young people found their way to the Universities of Paris and Oxford, they brought European ideas to Wales in French. This transference of thought was also promoted by the Cistercian houses.

In view of the high status of the Welsh language and the lively cultural background it is not surprising that the first *Eisteddfod* of which we have a fairly full record was held under the auspices of Rhys. Held at Cardigan in 1176, it was proclaimed a year beforehand in Ireland and Scotland as well as in Wales. The chair for poetry was won by a northerner while the victorious musician was a southerner.

The tomb of Rhys ap Gruffudd at St David's cathedral

Gerald the Welshman,
Three-quarters Norman

Giraldus Cambrensis, grandson of Princess Nest, wrote two unique books about Wales in splendid Latin which are an invaluable source of detailed knowledge of Wales in the time of Rhys ap Gruffudd. One was written after he toured Wales with Archbishop Baldwin who sought with some success to recruit men for the crusade. We learn for example that the Welsh could thank God even then that they were a musical nation. Gerald says that their mastery of three musical instruments, the harp, the fiddle and the pipes, was amazing. 'It appears,' he said, 'that the most perfect part of their art is its concealment.' But it was their vocal music that made him most enthusiastic:

> In their vocal music they do not sing the songs in unison as in other countries, but in many voices and in many parts and keys. Therefore, such is the custom of this nation you will hear in a company of singers as many keys and varying voices as you will see of heads … and it is not through art but through age-long custom in the course of prolonged time that this nation has won for itself their distinction.

Gerald's grandmother's Welsh blood ensured that he wrote fairly impartially about Wales, although his first loyalty was to the Normans. He could be severely critical of the Welsh and even advised the Norman king on the way to conquer Wales. This advice was followed by Edward I. Giraldus spent years as a student and then a lecturer in the University of Paris, where of course he worked in French, his native language. While he admired many

Welsh virtues he despised the English, preposterously declaring that 'The English are the most worthless people under the sun … In their own country the English are the slaves of the Normans, and of all slaves the most worthless … The English fight for greed, the Welsh for freedom.'

It was as warriors that he admired the Welsh most. 'Their mind,' he said, 'is solely on the defence of their country and their freedom. It is for their country that they fight, for freedom they labour, for these it seems sweet to them not only to fight with the sword but also to lay down their lives.'

And this characterises the whole nation, says Gerald, the common people as well as the aristocrats: 'When the bugle of war sounds, the countryman rushes to arms with the same alacrity as the courtier from his court.'

Among the other characteristics admired by Giraldus were intellectual ability, self-confidence and the absence of beggars. I quote his words:

> These people, being of a sharp and acute intellect, and gifted with a rich and powerful understanding, excel in whatever studies they pursue.
>
> Nature has given not only to the highest, but also to the inferior classes of the people of this nation, a boldness and confidence in speaking and answering, even in the presence of their princes and chieftains.
>
> No one of this nation ever begs, for the houses of all are common to all; and they place liberality and hospitality above all other virtues.

The Fight for Welsh Church Freedom

One aspect of Welsh literary culture was harnessed to the struggle to gain for the Welsh Church independence from Canterbury, for the Church centred on Canterbury was the powerful ecclesiastical arm of the British state. That was a major purpose of the popular literary genre of biographies of the early Welsh saints. *The Life of St David* was written by Rhygyfarch, one of the four scholarly sons of Sulien of Llanbadarn, the greatest scholar of the age, who had spent five years in Scottish and eleven years in Irish centres of learning. The Normans had closed the highest offices of the Church to Welshmen. The political interception of Canterbury had even persuaded the Pope to excommunicate Rhys ap Gruffudd.

The cathedral at St. Davids', Pembrokeshire

The most dramatic episode in the struggle was Giraldus Cambrensis's fight to create an archbishopric in St David's. The struggle was initially provoked by the king's refusal to accept Giraldus's nomination as bishop by the canons of St David's. In a courageous five-year struggle, Gerald went four times to Rome to set the case before Innocent III, the formidable lawyer-Pope. On his third visit he gave the Pope a letter from Llywelyn the Great and his nobles, supporting St David's case. He had the courage to challenge the king and the Norman establishment of England. The Prince of Powys declared:

> Many and great are the wars that we Welsh have fought against England, but not one was greater and fiercer than his against the King and the Archbishop when he withstood the whole might of England for the honour of Wales.

The king's excuse was that the archdeacon was an unsafe man to put in the bishopric of Menevia because he was related to Rhys ap Gruffudd and to almost all the great men of Wales. To promote a man of so noble a lineage, he said, would give new strength to the Welsh and would swell their pride. In the end, king John declared Gerald a traitor and all who supported him enemies of the English crown. Gerald's noble struggle for the independence of the Welsh Church gives him a claim to a place among the heroes of the two-century fight for freedom from Norman control.

Rhys ap Gruffudd had accompanied Gerald some years earlier on a part of his tour of Wales with Archbishop Baldwin. Rhys was by then very much the senior statesman, strong and chivalrous, courteous and hospitable, earning the epithet Rhys Mwynfawr (Most Benign). The Chronicle of the Princes describes him as 'gentle of speech, just and civilised to everyone'. But with the death of Henry II his détente with the crown comes to an end. The deteriorating relations compelled Rhys to safeguard his borders against the Marcher Lords. King Richard I sent an army led by his brother John towards Deheubarth, but to little effect. Discord among his sons caused him far greater trouble. But when he was in his sixties the glory of Rhys flamed again. He threw himself against Carmarthen, the royal centre, and burned it to the ground. Two years later he moved east to protect his north-eastern borders against aggressive Marcher Lords. Crossing the uplands of Builth he reduced the castle of Colwyn, the region's main fortress, and then crushed the combined forces of two powerful Marcher Lords. William de Breos would have suffered a similar fate if he had not come to an agreement. His borders now safe, Rhys returned to Dinefwr, and died in the following year.

In over half a century of struggle Rhys had succeeded in restoring and defending his heritage. His success, which was achieved in terrain far more difficult to defend than Gwynedd, was of massive importance to the whole of Wales. If southern Wales had suffered the fate of the Welsh-speaking kingdoms of the Old North, from Elfed to Ystrad Clud (Strathclyde), the Welsh language, which has maintained the nationhood of Wales, could with time have been completely lost. It is quite likely that if the old kingdom of Deheubarth and the rest of southern Wales had been under strong Norman-English government from the middle of the twelfth century on, the Welsh nation would, century by century, have faded away as the native language died. It was the prestige of Rhys ap Gruffudd, among the Normans as well as the Welsh, which ensured that the high status of the Welsh language would endure in southern Wales.

European Fame of the Glorious King Arthur

The book which dominated the twelfth century in Wales and beyond was the amazing work of Geoffrey of Monmouth, bishop of St Asaph, *Historia Regum Britanniae* (History of the Kings of Britain), translated many times into Welsh under the title *Brut y Brenhinedd* (The Chronicle of the Kings). Described by Halydan Koht as 'the most famous work of nationalistic historiography in the Middle Ages', it claims to give the history of Britain under Brythonic rule up to the time of Cadwaladr the Great. Although most of it is legendary, it was accepted for centuries as true history. Because of the splendid origins it attributed to the Brythons (Britons), and its fervent nationalist tone, the book was profoundly influential in Wales, adding cubits to the stature of the Welsh people in the time of Rhys ap Gruffudd and for centuries afterwards. But it was celebrated far beyond Wales and England. Its fame extended throughout Europe as far as the Middle East, largely because of its fascinating supposed history of the heroic King Arthur whose Round Table was at Caerleon.

It is possible that features from the lives of two other great military leaders were attributed to the legendary, as distinct from the historical, Arthur. One is the Brittanic commander Riothamus who responded to the appeal of the Emperor Anthemius for help in the Roman struggle against the Saxons by leading an army of twelve thousand to Gaul. He destroyed the Saxon army near the River Loire, but was defeated by the Visigoths. When he was retreating towards Avalon he disappeared, never to be seen again. The similarity between this and Geoffrey of Monmouth's assertion that Arthur's greatest exploit was to lead an army to the continent and to leave Sir Lancelot grieving as he was taken over the water to Avalon.

The other leader whose feats may have been attributed to Arthur was Emrys Wledig (Ambrosius Aurelianus) who recaptured London and Colchester, reconquered the Ickenfield Way, the strategic road between Reading and Cambridge, and prevented the Saxons from making further settlements.

Prince Llywelyn Fawr ('the Great')

In the opinion of the great historian J.E. Lloyd, the ablest of the series of gifted Welsh princes who ruled during the two centuries of Cymric-Norman wars was Llywelyn ap Iorwerth. His ability was made manifest by his mastery of a colonialism even harsher than that which faced his predecessors. Although he was the heir to eastern Gwynedd he had to defeat his uncle Dafydd before he could take possession of it. However, he inherited western Gwynedd peacefully on the death of his cousin Gruffudd in the first year of the thirteenth century, and would rule it for a further forty years. His authority extended from the Dovey estuary to the Dee. Powys lay along most of his eastern border, under the rule of the able and ambitious prince Gwenwynwyn. This ambition enabled king John to follow a policy of divide and rule, supporting Llywelyn at one time and then Gwenwynwyn another.

Five years after peacefully inheriting western Gwynedd, Llywelyn's status was confirmed by his marriage to John's illegitimate daughter, Joan. When John seized the territories of

William de Breos, one of the two most powerful Marcher Lords, Llywelyn grasped the opportunity given him to possess the southern half of Powys known as Powys Gwenwynwyn. His subsequent expulsion of Gwenwynwyn's ally Maelgwn from north Ceredigion indicated his hope of putting the whole of independent Wales under Gwynedd rule. But to avoid outraging his

Llywelyn ap Iorwerth

father-in-law, king John, he supported John's invasion of Scotland just as Alexander I of Scotland had joined the invasion of Gwynedd by Henry I three generations earlier. Nevertheless, John by now had concluded that Llywelyn was a dangerous enemy.

A second invasion by John with a very powerful force reached the Menai Straits and restricted Llywelyn's rule to western Gwynedd. The lesser Welsh princes withdrew their support for Llywelyn and accepted the overlordship of the English king. However, when John's tyrannical rule became unbearable and his intention to subjugate the Welsh became obvious, they renewed their allegiance to Llywelyn. Royal castles such as Aberystwyth were burnt, eastern Gwynedd was regained and Marcher Lordships were attacked. The Pope supported the insurgent Welsh and encouraged Philip Augustus of France to make Llywelyn an ally. John's response to this was to gather a large force at Chester with the intention of crushing Llywelyn finally. The invasion was halted, however, partly by the intervention of Llywelyn's wife Joan with whom her father John had a good relationship, and partly by the hostility of the barons. John vented his frustration by killing a number of his Welsh hostages, including Maelgwn's seven year old son.

The barons' anger increased, particularly after the failure of John's attempt to reconquer Normandy. Llywelyn of course exploited the situation. His capture of Shrewsbury in 1215 was a notable help in persuading John to sign the Magna Carta. In Wales, Llywelyn and his allies captured Carmarthen which had been a royal centre for sixty years. The major castles taken by Llywelyn and his allies included Cydweli, Llansteffan, St Clears, Laugharne, Narberth and Trefdraeth and, after Christmas, Cardigan and Cilgerran castles were also captured. Of all the major castles of the south-west, Pembroke and Haverfordwest alone remained in Norman hands. Deeply-entrenched Norman power was imperilled as far as Brecon.

Llywelyn was now strong enough to demand and receive the homage of the rulers of Powys Fadog, Powys Gwenwynwyn, Deheubarth, Buellt, Maeliennydd, Gwent and Glamorgan – virtually the whole of the remainder of Wales. When Gwenwynwyn broke his oath of allegiance his territory was seized by Llywelyn. It was then that he called a national senate at Aberdyfi to decide on the way to share the southern kingdom of Deheubarth among the factious descendants of Rhys ap Gruffudd.

Both king John and Prince Gwenwynwyn died in 1216.

The new Norman regime was free from the fierce baronial opposition which John had faced. Although it recognised Gwynedd's supremacy, and although it permitted Llywelyn to keep Carmarthen and Cardigan castles and the territory of Powys Gwenwynwyn, he was not allowed to continue to receive the homage of the lords of Deheubarth and Powys.

Five years later the crown officials once more tried to restrict Llywelyn's power to Gwynedd. William, earl of Pembroke, rector of the kingdom of England, brought a strong force over from Ireland which captured Carmarthen and Cardigan castles. Hubert de Burgh, justiciar of England, built a stronger castle at Montgomery, but his attempt to seize commotes in Powys was heavily defeated by Llywelyn in the battle of Ceri, in which William de Breos was taken prisoner.

De Breos's captivity led to an extraordinary personal drama. During his imprisonment de Breos and Joan, Llywelyn's wife, became lovers and were discovered together in bed by Llywelyn. Both were imprisoned. Soon the magnates of England and Wales were stunned by the news that William de Breos had been publicly hanged in the presence of eight hundred men, ending the de Breos empire. The muted response to this grim but intrepid act reflected Llywelyn's power.

When William de Burgh did win some Marcher Lordships, Llywelyn led a campaign in 1231 in which he burned Brecon, marched through Caerleon and Glamorgan, destroyed the Norman centre at Neath and as a culminating success seized Cardigan castle. Henry III appealed in vain to Ireland for help.

When the Norman barons once more became hostile to the crown, Llywelyn sided with them. In the ensuing peace agreement his position was restored to the situation as it was at the end of John's reign. He ruled Powys Gwenwynwyn, Builth, Gwrtheyrnion and Maeliennydd, which composed most of mid-Wales, and his authority was regained in Deheubarth and Powys Fadog. No Welsh prince had achieved such power in the Norman period.

Gwynedd's overlordship was now accepted by the Welsh princes and lords, even to the extent of accepting Llywelyn's eldest son Dafydd as his heir in a 'parliament' of nobles meeting at Strata Florida. Two years later Llywelyn died in the Cistercian monastery of Aberconwy where he had taken monk's habit in his last days. The Welsh Cistercians, the order of the White monks, had long become, says T.J. O'Sullivan, 'not only nationally conscious, but nationalistic as well'. But when his wife Joan died three years earlier and was buried at Llanfaes in Ynys Môn, it was to the Franciscans that Llywelyn gave land to build a monastery there. This would be burnt down by English forces nearly two centuries later because of the monks' support for Owain Glyndŵr.

In his tribute to the great prince, Sir J.E. Lloyd says, 'No man made better or more judicious use of the native force of the Welsh people for adequate national ends; his patriotic statesmanship will always entitle him to wear the proud title of Llywelyn the Great.'

Prince Llywelyn ap Gruffudd
Fights to the Death

Llywelyn Fawr was followed by his heir Dafydd, a man of notable ability, in accord with the agreement made at the Strata Florida 'Parliament'. Though the size and status of Gwynedd were again reduced, Dafydd proclaimed himself Prince of Wales. In his six-year reign he proved himself a worthy successor of his father, recovering territory in many parts of the land. In order to secure the independence of his principality he requested the Pope to permit him to hold Wales as a papal vassal in the way a number of European leaders did. Then tragedy befell Gwynedd and Wales. Exhausted by two winters of ferocious war against the armies of Henry III, during which the king commanded the killing of more than a score of Welsh hostages – including the son of Ednyfed Fychan, Llywelyn ap Gruffudd's seneschal – Dafydd died.

Llywelyn II, grandson of Llywelyn the Great, and his brother Owain had immediately to face three years of bitter warfare against Henry III's forces and were compelled to accept an agreement in 1247 which demoted Gwynedd greatly in size and status. But Llywelyn amazingly recovered strength. He regained eastern Gwynedd and in 1256–58 swept through Wales, taking possession of Merioneth, Builth and Gwrtheyrnion, expelling the hostile prince of lower Powys and persuading the prince of upper Powys to transfer his allegiance from Henry III to himself. In the same period his allies among the grandsons of Rhys ap Gruffudd seized control of Ceredigion and Ystrad Tywi.

After a short Christmas stay at home, Llywelyn again set out for Powys where he penetrated the Severn Valley and occupied the land as far as Trallwng (Welshpool). From there he proceeded to Glamorgan where he won the support of the Welsh of Gower. Before returning to Gwynedd for Easter he won the support of Cydweli and Carnwyllion where the Normans had been particularly strong. In May he was in Powys again, winning a victory near Llanfyllin.

It was at the end of that month of May that the men of Deheubarth won one of the greatest of Welsh victories. A strong Norman army left Carmarthen with the intention of re-occupying Dinefwr. When they reached the environs of the castle they were harassed mercilessly for two days. On the second of June they were compelled to retreat. But with the Welsh attacking them all the way they failed to reach the safety of Carmarthen. The final battle of the campaign seems to have been fought at Y Cymerau, where the river Cothi joins the Tywi seven miles from Carmarthen. 'More than three thousand Englishmen fell that day,' wrote a chronicler at Talyllychau (Talley Abbey); 'very few if any of the armed knights survived the battle.'

Once again Henry III led an attack on Gwynedd, assembling his army at Chester and drawing a navy from the Cinque ports. Irish help had also been purchased. While Henry's army was waiting for its arrival, it was attacked ceaselessly by the Welsh and forced ignominiously to retreat. Llywelyn, who now had a fleet of his own, may himself have prevented the Irish from reaching Gwynedd. The Prince was now at the apex of his power, his energy, says Powicke, informed by intelligence, and his footmen supplemented by bodies of heavily armed horse-soldiers.

Llywelyn sought help outside Wales. He allied himself with the national party in Scotland. The earl of Monteith gave the bishop of Bangor, who acted as Llywelyn's messenger, a document in which the Scots undertook to make no separate peace with the king of England and to give him no aid against the Welsh, but trade between the Scots and the Welsh was to be encouraged. In the following year the rulers of Powys, Deheubarth and Glamorgan recognised Llywelyn not only as their leader but also as their lord, thus indicating their will that Wales should live as a nation. But the Norman-English determined otherwise. They had the power and wealth to work their will on the Welsh.

Llywelyn is Recognised as Prince of Wales

Although his relations with the king had deteriorated, and although his astonishing run of victories had humiliated Henry III's son Edward unbearably, Llywelyn's position was strengthened by an alliance with the most powerful baron of the day, Simon de Montfort, into whose hands the king and government had fallen. Simon recognised him as prince of Wales. Llywelyn suffered a very heavy blow, however, a short while later when de Montfort was killed in the battle of Evesham. Although the hostile Marcher Lords were strengthened by this, Llywelyn, undaunted, won a series of victories against them.

Two years after de Montfort's death, Henry III felt compelled to acknowledge his power. The Treaty of Montgomery which Henry signed in 1267 recognised Llywelyn as the Prince of Wales who had the right to the homage of all Welsh lords except the lord of Dryslwyn. He was allowed to retain all the gains he had made in the previous years and to prove his right to other Marcher Lordships. Although Llywelyn was still a vassal of the king of England, the principality of Wales had all the marks of full nationhood. Its political order now seemed to be strong enough to defend and sustain its national civilisation against the overbearing power of the comparatively huge centralised neighbouring state.

Llywelyn built the castle of Dolforwyn and the town of Abermule near Montgomery in central Wales, hoping to establish an administrative centre there for the whole of Wales, and he sought to increase his power in the areas where he was weakest. The strong support given him by the lord of Senghennydd, which extended from Brecon to within a few miles of Cardiff, threatened the territory of Gilbert de Clare, earl of Gloucester and lord of Glamorgan. Indeed, Llywelyn had just defeated an army of knights there. Consequently, de Clare built a castle at Caerffili. It was destroyed by Llywelyn in 1271, to be replaced by a mighty structure second only to Windsor castle in size, such was the Norman fear of Llywelyn's power.

However, Llywelyn's position changed for the worst with the accession of monoglot French-speaking Edward I to the 'English' throne. The new king – who had been humiliated more than once by Llywelyn on the battlefield – was a harsher imperialist even than his predecessors. His objective was clear. Seeing the war as a contest between two countries, one an imperial kingdom of enormous power, the other a diminutive principality, fragile and puny in comparison, he was determined, says the historian Tout, to wipe out the Welsh by making them English, who were despised by the Normans. His tactics appear to be designed to that end.

For instance, Edward seized the ship in which Elinor de Montfort, Llywelyn's distinguished wife by proxy, was sailing from France to Wales, and imprisoned her in Windsor castle for three years. As the differences between Edward and Llywelyn multiplied, the Welsh prince refused to do homage to Edward in person until the king considered his host of complaints. Matters came to a head in 1276 when Edward embarked on immense and costly preparations to invade Wales and destroy the Welsh political order. A force of eight hundred knights and fifteen thousand foot soldiers moved into mountainous Gwynedd, while Ynys Môn's grain harvest, on which the people of Gwynedd relied, was reaped and seized by Edward's men. As the war continued through the winter, refuge became impossible for Llywelyn's men because of lack of food and pasture. After a long and bitter amphibious war in which Edward was personally involved, he succeeded in breaking Llywelyn and destroying the principality. The financial cost was enormous. Gwyn Alf Williams says that Edward had to mortgage the crown to Italian bankers and mobilise the merchants. In addition he initiated a revolutionary change in English military society.

Once again Gwynedd's territory was reduced to the west of Conwy and its status was sorely diminished, although the title Prince of Wales was retained. That his dignity remained is indicated by his marriage to Elinor de Montfort in Worcester Cathedral in the presence of the kings and queens of England and Scotland. He diligently observed the harsh terms of the Treaty of Aberconwy made after his defeat, which included Edward's occupation of large tracts of Wales such as northern Ceredigion, where he built a very strong castle at Aberystwyth, as he did in

Flint, Rhuddlan and Builth to protect areas in his possession.

The people, however, writhed under Edward's oppressive rule. The imposition of English law was particularly detested. A colonialist campaign was led by Pecham, Archbishop of Canterbury, against the Welsh, whom he scorned as barbarous and blasphemous. He demanded 'the elimination of the independence of the Welsh and their incorporation into the civilised orbit of English law'. It was the oppression of Edward and the Marcher Lords which provoked Dafydd, Llywelyn's brother, to rebel and launch the last great struggle for freedom from Norman government.

War was declared in a parliament held at Denbigh. Morale was high, with most of the Welsh princes united in support of Dafydd. On Palm Sunday, 21 March 1282, Hawarden castle was seized. The following day Oswestry was ravaged. The north-east and Powys were ignited. Rhuddlan castle was captured and so was Builth castle in mid Wales. The war spread to Ceredigion; Aberystwyth castle was seized. By 26 March Ystrad Tywi was aflame. Llandovery and Carreg Cennen castles were captured by the lords of Deheubarth who also heavily defeated the army of Gilbert de Clare, Edward's commander in southern Wales, in a battle near Dinefwr on 16 June.

Llywelyn was weighing the pros and cons of throwing himself into the conflict when Elinor died on the birth of their daughter Gwenllïan on 19 June 1282. This personal tragedy probably influenced his ultimate decision that his support for the rising was imperative. Edward reacted with the same strategy as in the 1277 war. Proclaiming his will 'to put an end finally … to the malice of the Welsh', he mobilised massive resources from the length and breadth of his empire. The costs were no less than seven times as great as the immense expenditure he incurred in 1277. Despite that, he was compelled personally to spend months in Wales to terminate the Welsh resistance once and for all. The uplands between the rivers Wye and Severn were doggedly defended, dashing Edward's hopes of crossing the north-east quickly. Most humiliating of all was the battle of Moel-y-don in which the Welsh overwhelmed a large force under the command of Luc de Tany, seneschal of Gascony, who had been sent to subdue Ynys Môn (Anglesey). Hundreds were killed or drowned when trying to cross the Menai Straits on a bridge of boats.

Ah God, that the Sea would Cover the Land

Norman forces had violated a truce which had been arranged to enable Archbishop Pecham to mediate between Edward and Llywelyn. In early November 1282 Pecham was at Llywelyn's headquarters at Aber near the Menai coast discussing the relations between the king and the prince. When the king, through Pecham, offered Llywelyn an earldom in England, the prince replied that the plan had astounded 'everyone who had heard of it, for its purpose was to destroy and undermine my people and myself rather than to offer me honour and safety'. Llywelyn insisted on the undeniable rights of the Welsh nation which, he affirmed, was a nation different from England in language, law and customs, and he proclaimed the right of the Welsh to defend these essentials, observing that in doing so they were defending their freedom.

About the same time Pecham received a letter from the nobles of Gwynedd stating that:

> The prince should not throw aside his inheritance and that of his ancestors in Wales and accept land in England, with whose language, way of life, laws and customs he is unfamiliar... Let this be clearly understood: his council will not permit him to yield... and even if the prince wishes to transfer [his people] into the hands of the king, they will not do any homage to any stranger as they are wholly unacquainted with his language, his way of life and his laws.

Pecham responded with an expression of loathing for the laws of Wales as the work of the devil, and declared that conquest alone could deliver the Welsh from their sloth and barbarity.

The Welsh victory at Moel-y-don had hardened Edward's resolve to crush Llywelyn, but it had also made it necessary for him to find still more men, money and resources, forcing him into a colossal debt which would have extensive consequences. But the daily growth of Anglo-Norman power compelled Llywelyn also to find new resources. It was possibly that, and the need to open a new front, which caused him to lead a part of his army through Powys to the Buellt area in mid-winter. Or perhaps he was inveigled by a treacherous invitation from the sons of Roger Mortimer, the powerful Marcher Lord with whom he had made an accord a year earlier. Among the letters of Archbishop Pecham there is said to be a document found on Llywelyn's body which refers to invitations from the Marcher Lords to go to the Builth district.

If Llywelyn was known to be coming, leaving his brother Dafydd to defend Gwynedd, the defeat of his force on the upland of Llanganten, reported in the *Chronicle of the Princes*, is more easily understood. Llywelyn himself was killed near the banks of the River Irfon, by a Shropshire knight who did not recognise him. The date was 11 December. When his body was recognised it was decapitated. His head was sent to London and paraded under a crown of ivy through the streets of the English capital to the accompaniment of horns and trumpets. The White monks carried his headless body for burial at Cwm-hir Abbey. So ended the life of a brave and cultured man who for more than a quarter of a century had with remarkable skill led his people's fight for freedom.

Llywelyn's death ended an epoch. 1282, says *Brenhinedd y Saeson,* was the year when 'the whole of Wales was thrown to the ground'. Cymru was one in its grief. The bards were fully aware of the enormity of the disaster. Gruffudd ab yr Ynad Coch, in one of the greatest European elegies of the Middle Ages, saw the cosmos itself immersed in the flood of grief. The one hundred and eight lines of the elegy, composed in the complicated *cynghanedd* tradition, turn on a single rhyme. A translation of the ten lines below gives some concept of its nature:

Llywelyn ap Gruffudd

See you not the rush of wind and rain?
See you not the oaks lash each other?
See you not the ocean scourging the shore?
See you not the truth is portending?
See you not the sun hurtling through the sky?
See you not that the stars have fallen?
Have you no belief in God, foolish men?
See you not that the world is ending?
Ah God, that the sea would cover the land!
What is left us that we linger?

Despite the utter and unrelieved despair caused by Llywelyn's death, the two centuries of struggle was not yet finally ended. It continued for a further seven months under Llywelyn's brother, prince Dafydd, an able and courageous warrior who took the title Prince of Wales. Although the most important military activities were in Gwynedd, the lords of Deheubarth played a worthy part. An English army moved up the Conwy valley and, after a campaign lasting three weeks, captured Dafydd's stronghold at Dolwyddelan. Another force crossed from Ynys Môn, seized Caernarfon castle and then Harlech. Dafydd moved his court to the Dysynni valley on the southern side of Cader Idris where Castell y Bere, the handsome castle built by Llywelyn Fawr, was the last effective bastion of resistance. When it fell to an army of four thousand men, Dafydd returned to Dolbadarn in the Conwy valley.

Among those who stood with prince Dafydd to the last were Hywel ap Rhys Grŷg, a descendant of the great Rhys ap Gruffudd, prince of Deheubarth, and Goronwy ap Heilyn who had been Llywelyn's and was now Dafydd's seneschal. It is right to recall their loyalty. With the capture of the prince on 28 June the

71

French-speaking Normans completed their last European conquest, more than two hundred years after their conquest of England.

The fate of Dafydd, Llywelyn the Great's last grandson, was to be dragged through the streets of Shrewsbury on a gibbet tied to horses' tails; then hanged, disembowelled and quartered. Four favoured English towns were each given a quarter. London received his head, which was placed beside Llywelyn's skull at the Tower of London. His two sons, Owain and Llywelyn, were incarcerated in Bristol castle where they remained until they died, while his daughter Gwladys was sent to a Lincolnshire nunnery where she died a year before Llywelyn's daughter Gwenllïan died in a neighbouring nunnery at Sempringham.

An English historian wrote, 'The history of Wales now comes to an end.' But it was not so.

Edward I's Wales

Edward spent most of the two years after the conquest in Wales, which was still neither incorporated into England nor governed by the English parliament. The king lacked the power to abolish the Marcher Lordships. In fact, he added to their number as a reward for the Lords' help in conquering Wales. The whole of Wales was not dissimilar to one great March of which large parts were in the possession of the king himself. It was not a part of England but largely a separate possession of the English crown and governed by royal statute. Commotes remained under the administration of sheriffs, whose offices were filled, like all important posts, by Englishmen. Welsh criminal law was abolished but Welsh civil law remained. Welshmen were never to be tried under Welsh criminal or civil law and never in the Welsh language. Every Welsh person could be excluded from the eighty towns in Wales as foreigners.

The steep rise in taxes caused great distress, especially among the *taeogion* (villeins), whose taxes were increased by six hundred per cent and more. Edward said that this was necessary to pay the tremendous cost of the war and the immense castle-building programmes in the post-war years and after the dangerously powerful Welsh revolt twelve years later. Dr John Davies says that Edward's activities in Wales cost him more than ten times his regular annual income, and that his massive Welsh-incurred debt vitiated his hope of subjugating the Scots.

James of St.George, the great architect who designed some of the castles, maintained, says Dr Davies, that the king's hold on Wales could not be secured without the most elaborate fortifications, for 'Welshmen are Welshmen'. The huge and costly castles underline Gerald the Welshman's dictum about the Welsh a century before: 'Their mind is wholly on the defence of their country and its freedom.' Although the castles are badges of subjugation they are also a tribute to the Welsh determination to live in freedom.

A bigger anglicising influence than the castles themselves were the towns which developed around them, each one an alien colony in which Welsh people were forbidden to live or to trade. As a poet sang at that time:

> Lle bu'r Brython Saeson sydd
> A'r boen ar Gymru beunydd.
>
> *Where once were Britons, English now*
> *give the Welsh daily pain.*

Planting scores of urban English colonies all over Wales furthered Edward's policy, if the historian Tout is right in saying that the king's real policy was to make Welshmen Englishmen as soon as possible.

The Risings of Madog and Llywelyn Bren

It soon became obvious that Edward's oppression was bitterly hated and that the Welsh were far from being demoralised by the military conquest. Their spiritual defeat would not come for another three centuries, ironically after Henry Tudor's victory on Bosworth Field. The first two Welsh lords to rebel had themselves helped to create the system with which they were now sorely disillusioned. Rhys ap Maredudd of Dryslwyn, the only descendant of Rhys ap Gruffudd to support the king in Llywelyn's fight for freedom, rose in rebellion in the summer of 1287, less than five years after the conquest. He had been angered by the king's decision to take personal possession of the old royal Welsh fortress of Dinefwr, and the greater part of the territories of members of the house of Deheubarth, instead of rewarding Rhys for his support. He captured the castles of Dinefwr and Llandovery, and Carreg Cennen on its defiant precipice. Then he attacked Carmarthen and Llanbadarn fifty miles to the north. Powerful armies had to be brought in from England to defeat him. Rhys was besieged in Dryslwyn castle for three weeks by a force of twelve thousand men, but he escaped to the mountains. After being a hunted man for four years he was caught and executed at York.

In 1294, three years after the execution of Rhys ap

Maredudd, there was a far more dangerous rebellion in which the Welsh had planned to rise in different parts of the country when it was thought Edward would be in France. When they did rise, however, Edward with a big army was still at Portsmouth before the wind rose. Madog ap Llywelyn, a descendant of Owain Gwynedd, rose in Gwynedd, Maelgwn in Ceredigion, Cynan in Brycheiniog (Brecon) and Morgan in Glamorgan. It was a national insurrection. On one day there were attacks on castles as far apart as Caernarfon and Cardigan, Denbigh and Castell y Bere, and Builth. By October, the whole of Gwynedd was in the hands of the Welsh, and over in the Clwyd valley Henry de Lacy, a powerful Marcher Lord, was defeated.

Edward assembled enormous resources and an army of 35,000 men to reconquer Wales, where he had to spend another nine months. He reached Conwy by Christmas but was held up there for weeks by the Welsh defence. Madog had to leave the siege of Edward's army in Conwy in order to find new allies in Powys. There, however, he was killed by the earl of Warwick's army in the battle of Caereinion. This was followed by the most horrific act of the war, the killing of five hundred Welshmen in their sleep.

Despite the venomous oppression imposed by the Anglo-Normans, thousands of Welshmen made a living by serving in their armies. The victorious army in the battle of Caereinion, like all England's armies in this period, contained a large contingent of Welshmen who were masters of the deadly long bow. These men were responsible for a number of important English victories and were usually dressed in a national uniform of green and white. In Edward's Flanders campaign 5,300 Welshmen served, 4,000 in Gascony, 5,000 in the battle of Crécy, and of 12,500 of Edward's foot soldiers at the battle of Falkirk 10,500 were Welsh.

After Madog's death Edward's forces moved through Wales without danger. Two southern leaders, Cynan and Morgan, were captured and executed. But the alarm caused by the rising accelerated Edward's castle-building programme. In 1301 the king tried to mollify the Welsh by investing his son Edward, who had been born in Caernarfon in 1294, as Prince of Wales, and assigned to him all the king's territories in Wales, known as the principality.

But the south was not calm for long; the oppression suffered was too heavy. For instance, after Gilbert de Clare was killed at Bannockburn, Payne de Turbeville, who succeeded him as Lord of Glamorgan, advocated the expulsion of Welsh people from his Lordship. The vicious discrimination against the native Welsh in the English boroughs, and the alien settlement in the Vale of Glamorgan, were a continuing tyranny. The bad harvests of 1316–18 aggravated the situation.

When the Glamorgan men could bear no more they turned to their natural leader, Llywelyn Bren. Llywelyn was a nobleman whose father had been a staunch supporter of Prince Llywelyn II. Described by a chronicler as 'a great man and powerful in his country', he was descended from Princess Nest, daughter of Rhys ap Tewdwr king of Deheubarth, and from Ifor Bach, lord of Senghennydd, who was known for his daredevil attack on Cardiff castle. Llywelyn Bren went to ask Edward II for help but was given a very hostile reception. He therefore shouldered the leadership of the men of Glamorgan, together with his five sons.

Rising in 1314, they attacked a number of towns from Newport in the east to Kenfig in the west. The huge Caerffili castle was the first castle to be attacked. The chief officials were taken captive and Caerffili town was destroyed. The king, fearing a repetition of the Madog ap Llywelyn rising, responded swiftly, gathering forces from all parts of Wales and the Marches as indications of a widespread rising increased. The men of Ystrad Tywi rose in sympathy and burnt the borough of Dinefwr while Llywelyn Bren attacked Cardiff and Caerleon.

Once again however English resources proved too great. A two-pronged attack drove Llywelyn westwards beyond the Rhondda valley after raising the siege on Caerffili castle. Llywelyn had intended making a stand at Ystradfellte near the top of the Neath valley; this was on 18 March, two months after the rising began. But he decided that it would be wrong to sacrifice his men in a battle against overwhelming odds. He told his followers, 'I started this course of events. I will put myself in their hands so that the people may be spared. It is better that one man die than that the whole population be put to the sword.' After being held in the Tower of London for a year he was brought to Cardiff. There he was hanged, drawn and quartered. Pieces of his body were distributed among the Glamorgan boroughs as a warning to Welshmen tempted to try to win freedom from oppression.

Llywelyn Bren, a cultured man, was one of the class of *uchelwyr* (great men) which replaced the less numerous courts of the princes as sponsors of culture. The *uchelwyr*, who were confidently proud of their national identity, were the patrons of the splendid bards of the next three centuries. The bards were often political leaders. It was they who did most to develop political nationalism. The fourteenth-century poet Dafydd ap Gwilym was the brightest star in the brilliant Welsh literary firmament and indeed the supreme poetic genius of the Celtic nations. Born in north Ceredigion some sixty years after the conquest, he was the son of one of the most influential noble families in Dyfed, very much at home in the Cymric-Norman society of the time. Like all the great bards he travelled Wales from end to end, from Ynys Môn to Gwent, visiting friends and patrons. His greatest friend was Ifor Hael (Ivor the Generous) who lived in Maesaleg (Bassaleg) near Newport, Gwent.

Dafydd ap Gwilym sang mainly of nature and the love of women. Iolo Goch called him 'The hawk of the girls of Deheubarth'. His passionate love of life and of nature flows through all his love poems. It is his splendid nature poetry which gives him his unique place in medieval poetry. The great authority on Dafydd's work is Sir Thomas Parry, who says:

> The unending wonder in Dafydd ap Gwilym's work is this: however overflowing his poetic energy – the ideas bubbling in his head, the images wrestling for expression, every sinew extended to the uttermost to express the great splendour of his mistress – he never relaxes his grip on his craft or forgets the design and pattern of his poem. His mastery of his medium is always without blemish, his restraint and his discipline always consistent.

Owain of the Red Hand, the Deliverer

Another patriotic fourteenth century character, but totally different from Llywelyn Bren and Dafydd ap Gwilym, was Owain Lawgoch (Owain of the Red Hand). Owain ap Thomas ap Rhodri was very much involved in the fight for Welsh freedom, although his home for most of his life was in France where at twenty years of age he joined the service of Philip VI, king of France. Known as Yvain de Galles, 'the prodigious Owain', as

Barbara Tuchman calls him, earned a big reputation as a brilliant leader of professional military forces, securing a place in the folk literature of France, Brittany, Switzerland, Lombardy and the Channel Islands. Sometimes he commanded his own independent force with such Welsh lieutenants as Owain ap Rhys and Ieuan Wyn, who was known as *Poursuivant D'Amour*.

Owain Lawgoch had long claimed to be the heir of Llywelyn II's principality, and when war broke out again between France and England, king Philip, conscious of his debt to Owain for some of his victories, and seeing at the same time a way of embarrassing England, decided to help him regain his heritage. A fleet was assembled in Harfleur in 1369 to sail for Wales, but storms held it back. The English defence of Wales, where Owain's name had excited hope, was put in the hands of the Duke of Lancaster while Sir Gregory Sais, a Welshman, commanded the six most powerful castles of the south-west. Meanwhile, in 1372, Owain was given three hundred thousand francs by the king of France to finance his Welsh campaign. His hopes of success were increased when the French destroyed an English fleet near La Rochelle and by the knowledge that preparations to receive him were being made by supporters in Gwynedd.

Owain issued a proclamation which declared his right to be the prince of Wales as a descendant of its kings, and that Charles, the powerful king of France, 'has given me the aid and support of his army and fleet to recover the land which is my rightful patrimony'. He sailed for Wales from Harfleur with an army of four thousand – bigger than the French army which a generation later landed at Milford Haven to support Owain Glyndŵr, and twice the size of Henry Tudor's army which came to Milford from Brittany sixty years after that. Owain's force reached Guernsey where, according to French historians, four hundred of the enemy were killed in a battle against the English. For centuries Owain's name lingered there in story and song. But a crisis in La Rochelle compelled the French king to recall the force.

Owain had not abandoned hope. The English government feared an invasion eight years later. They decided that Owain must be assassinated because, says Froissart the great French historian, 'this Yvain de Galles was greatly hated in England'. After the Royal Council of England had formally required his murder, a plot was hatched by the English officials in Bordeaux. The name of the hired assassin was John Lamb. Purporting to sympathise with Owain, and on the pretext of bringing him good news from Wales, he won Owain's trust and was made his personal chamberlain. One morning in October 1478, during the siege of the castle of Montegne sur Mer, Owain was sitting in front of the castle with Lamb behind him combing his hair. Suddenly the assassin plunged a dagger through his heart and fled to the castle. At the command of the king of England he was paid £20 for the job.

So died Owain, the chief hope of Welsh freedom at that time. Froissart, the contemporary French historian called the Herodotus of the Middle Ages, gives him considerable notice, describing Yvain de Galles as the flower of chivalry, irascible and pugnacious but gracious and generous of spirit. Within a little over two decades, another Owain, hoped to be the longed-for deliverer, would be making an agreement with the king of France and receiving his military aid in his fight for national freedom.

Owain Glyndŵr's War of Liberation

By far the most powerful struggle for national freedom after the Norman conquest was Glyndŵr's astonishing war of liberation in the first two decades of the fifteenth century. The tenacity of Glyndŵr and his men is amazing. Revolts of this kind in European countries, including Wales, did not usually last for more than a few months. Glyndŵr's war of liberation was aflame for ten years and did not finally end for fifteen. Behind the war lay the anger of people from all walks of life, but most particularly the poor, at the oppression they suffered. None were more alienated than the clerics, who were often men of noble families, for the Church was despotically used by the English government as a colonising weapon. Of the sixteen bishops promoted to Welsh bishoprics in the last quarter of the fourteenth century, only one was a Welshman. The shock given to the *uchelwyr* by the murder of Richard II, who was well-liked in northern Wales, also contributed to the turmoil. But above all it was a national insurrection.

Owain Glyndŵr had the lineage necessary to be a Welsh national leader. He was descended through his father from the last king of the whole of Powys, and through his mother he was in the royal line of the kingdom of Deheubarth. He was thought by the bards to be the *Mab Darogan* (the Son of Prophecy), the Deliverer, following Owain Lawgoch. Two lordships were in his hands, Glyndyfrdwy where he was born, and Cynllaith Owain. Groomed as a coming Cadwaladr he had the best education available with the sons of the English aristocracy in Westminster and the Inns of Court where the poet Chaucer was a contemporary. He married

Marged, daughter of the Cymricised Norman Sir David Hanmer, chief justice of the King's Bench.

There is no finer picture of a Welsh home in the literature of Wales than Iolo Goch's poem on Sycharth, Owain's home, composed about 1390. It is a home, whose setting is described in entrancing detail, where the grace of hospitality flourishes:

Owain Glyndŵr

> Anfynych iawn fu yno
> Weled na chlicied na chlo.
>
> *Seldom has there been seen there*
> *Either a latch or a lock.*

With him lived a splendid family – Marged his wife, six sons and three daughters:

> A gwraig orau o'r gwragedd …
> A'i blant a ddeuant bob ddau
> Nythaid teg o benaethau.
>
> *The best wife among women …*
> *His children come, two by two*
> *A fine nestful of princes.*

Such was the home of the man described by the historian G.M. Trevelyan as, 'This wonderful man, an attractive and unique figure in a period of debased and selfish politics.' Such was the home, burnt down by the enemy three years later, and such the man who left it in the first year of the fifteenth century to lead the fight for Welsh freedom. On 16 September in the year 1400, now celebrated as Glyndŵr Day, a group of prominent Welshmen, some of Norman-Welsh descent – including Gruffudd and Philip Hanmer, his wife's brothers, and Robert Puleston, his sister's husband – gathered at Glyndyfrdwy. The Dean of St Asaph represented the Welsh clerics. In a stirring revolutionary act they proclaimed Glyndŵr Prince of Wales. All this noble company remained faithful to their prince, some faithful unto death, throughout the coming war of liberation.

This carefully planned act had the support of all classes of society, from the powerful Tudors of Anglesey, Glyndŵr's cousins and ancestors of the Tudor royal family, to Welsh labourers who – according to a parliamentary report – returned from the fields in England to follow Owain. English students in Oxford shouted 'Slay, slay the Welsh dogs'. According to another parliamentary report a company of Welsh students met in the home of a certain Alice Walsh and 'with many wicked meetings and councils … planned against our Lord the king and the Realm for the destruction of the kingdom and the English language!' Students abandoned their studies and left for home to join Glyndŵr. One is reminded of Giraldus Cambrensis's words about the Welsh over two centuries earlier, 'Their mind is solely on the defence of their country and their freedom … When the bugle of war sounds the countryman rushes to arms with the same alacrity as the courtier from his court.'

The immediate cause of the rising was the theft of some of Glyndŵr's land by the Marcher Lord Grey, and Glyndŵr's humiliating failure to get justice in Parliament. When bishop John Trefor warned them of the possibly dire consequences they replied contemptuously, 'What care we for the barefoot rascals?'.

Owain Crowned Prince of Wales

Significantly, Glyndŵr's first attacks were on towns. Havoc was wrought on every town in north-east Wales including Rhuthun, Denbigh, Flint, Rhuddlan, Holt, Hawarden, Oswestry and Welshpool. Then rebellion was raised in Ynys Môn by Owain's cousins Rhys and Gwilym Tudor. The lower clergy joined the struggle, as did the Cistercians and Franciscans. As soon as October 1400, king Henry IV led a large army across northern Wales, burning and looting unmercifully but failing to capture any person of importance. The winter was spent by Owain with a small group of men in the mountains. Easter saw the Tudor brothers capturing Conwy castle, and weeks later Owain Glyndŵr won a vital victory on the Hyddgen Mountain in the Pumlumon range, opening up the road to the south. He wrote to Henry Don, the most powerful man in the Cydweli district, an ancestor of the poet John Don, 'We want you to know that through God's help and yours we hope to free the people of Wales from their servitude to our English enemies who have for a long time oppressed us and our ancestors.'

Once more Henry IV gathered his forces, terrorised the people and destroyed their food supplies. Otherwise his invasion was futile. He was present at the execution in Llandovery of Llywelyn ap Gruffudd of Caio, a prominent supporter of Owain's, described by Adam of Usk as a man 'of gentle birth and bountiful'. The execution in Cardiff of a man called Sperhauke indicated the variety of Glyndŵr's supporters, while a powerful attack on Caernarfon at the other end of the country showed the geographical extent of the war.

He was now strong enough to seek allies, first in the Celtic lands. In a letter written in French to Robert III of Scotland he reminded him that both of them were descended from the same Brythonic kings. 'The people of Wales,' he said, 'are under the oppressive bondage of your mortal enemies and mine, the English.' Help did come from Scotland. A similar letter, in Latin, was sent to the lords of Ireland, but its carrier was captured by the English. France was his most important ally by far. A letter from Glyndŵr to the king of France stated bluntly, 'My nation has been trampled underfoot by the barbarian English.' In 1401 Dafydd ap Ieuan Goch of Ceredigion, who had spent twenty years in the service of the king of Cyprus and other Mediterranean Christians, was sent by king Charles VI of France on Glyndŵr's behalf to the court of king Robert of Scotland. Unfortunately he too was caught by the English and incarcerated in the Tower of London.

Owain, however, continued to succeed without external aid. A series of notable victories greatly increased his power in 1402. In April of that year Lord Grey himself was taken prisoner, and under pressure from parliament the king had to pay a big ransom, which enriched Owain's coffers for his release. Although Henry Percy (Hotspur), who had overwhelmed the Scots a little earlier, was made chief officer of the Principality, Glyndŵr retained the initiative. When he attacked Maeliennydd, the northern half of Radnorshire, he won a brilliant victory at Brynglas near Knighton on the English border against a large English army from which Welsh bowmen crossed to the side of their fellow countrymen. A number of prominent English leaders died in the battle, but its most notable feature was the capture of Edmund Mortimer, the most powerful Marcher Lord, whose claim to the throne was stronger than Henry's. Brynglas completed the transformation of Glyndŵr's war from a series of skirmishes to a national uprising.

When the king refused to pay the ransom asked for Mortimer's release, Glyndŵr seized the opportunity with relish. Mortimer married his daughter Catrin, of whom Shakespeare's Mortimer says, 'her tongue makes Welsh as sweet as ditties highly penned'. Then he commanded his followers to support the Welsh cause. By now, with thousands of men in his forces, Glyndŵr was the master of Gwynedd and Powys and much of the rest of the land. His power extended even to the English border counties. A dramatic success was the adhesion of Henry Hotspur to his cause. The king was compelled to make a supreme effort to crush him. A massive force of a hundred thousand men was assembled in three huge armies, only to have their invasion weather-beaten back with the help of Welsh guerrillas. The king was heartened, however, when Hotspur was killed a fortnight later in the battle of Shrewsbury. Nevertheless, Glyndŵr continued to go from strength to strength. For the fourth time the king had to lead his hosts to Wales, reaching as far as Carmarthen to be forced to return by the Welsh guerrilla tactics, without a battle and without weakening Owain.

The major castles, the last centres of English power, were falling into Owain's hands. With eight thousand men behind him he seized the castles of Llansteffan, Newcastle Emlyn, Dryslwyn and Carreg Cennen. French warships attacked the castles of

Harlech, Beaumaris and Caernarfon in the north and ports in the south. Henry Don had their assistance in besieging Cydweli castle. Cardiff was burned to the ground and its castle captured. The men of the Gwent and Glamorgan hill country rose in Owain's support as they had done for Prince Llywelyn over a century before.

In 1404, the fourth year of the war, Glyndŵr won some of his biggest victories, including the capture of Harlech and Aberystwyth castles. The former was made his family's home and the location of his court for four years, while his treasury and civil service were in the latter. He was now served by an able body of civil servants and professional diplomats, including Gruffudd Young the chancellor, John Trefor, bishop of St Asaph, and Lewis Byford, bishop of Bangor. None sustained him more strongly than the priests of the Church and the members of the religious orders, the Franciscans, the Austinians and of course the Cistercians. The loyalty of these men to Wales was undivided.

Now that his mastery of Wales was complete Owain Glyndŵr called, in 1404, four from every commote in Wales to a parliament in Machynlleth. There, with the blessing of the Pope of Avignon and in the presence of envoys from France, Castile and Scotland, Glyndŵr was crowned 'Prince of Wales by the grace of God'. That was the description of Glyndŵr in the treaty made with France, signed in Paris by Gruffudd Young and John Hanmer and ratified by the Welsh parliament.

Wales now had her own state, with its civil servants and diplomats, its treasury and legal system, its armed forces, a Church whose independence of Canterbury was recognised by the Pope of Avignon, and a charismatic prince as head of state. Although the country was still full of hostile English military and civil people, Cymru had achieved a considerable measure of national freedom.

Two fundamental policies were proclaimed in the Pennal Parliament of 1406. One declared that the Welsh Church would be independent of Canterbury with Welsh-speaking priests and bishops and the archbishopric located at St David's. The other was that free Wales would have two universities, one in the south, the other in the north.

1405 was a year of mixed fortunes. The Welsh forces were twice defeated in Gwent, the first time near Grosmont and the second at Pwll Melyn near Usk on the English border. Glyndŵr's son Tudur was killed there and another son Gruffudd taken prisoner. Yet two developments showed the strength of Owain's position. One was the remarkable Tripartite Agreement made with his two chief English allies. This would have placed the north of England in the hands of the earl of Northumberland and the Percy family; the south, with the English crown, was to be Mortimer's. A free Wales under Glyndŵr would include the whole of the kingdom of Powys as it was in the seventh century, bounded by the Severn. The plan was foiled by the failure to smuggle Mortimer into Wales and the defeat of the earl of Northumberland's rising.

The other major event was the landing of three thousand French troops at Milford Haven. Glyndŵr met them with an army of ten thousand at his back, a tremendous logistical feat in a small country of about two hundred thousand people, little more than a fifteenth of England's population. The armies marched west, taking the town and castle in Haverfordwest and then Carmarthen thirty miles on. As they passed Caerleon, attention was drawn to 'the Round Table and Arthur's Majestic Abbey'. They marched over the border as far as Worcester, further into the heart of England than any foreign army had penetrated since 1066. After

Glyndŵr had returned to his own land, king Henry for the fifth time assembled large forces to invade Wales. Again the weather helped the Welsh to throw him back, leaving Owain in possession of valuable spoil.

Events turned against Owain from now on. The death of the earl of Northumberland was a bitter blow. Most of the French returned to France. Although Gruffudd Young and Bishop Byford of Bangor had been to Scotland that year because of the sympathetic interest the Scots had in the Glyndŵr war, their work was undone when the heir to the Scottish king was taken prisoner by the English. In the next year Louis of Orléans, Glyndŵr's greatest friend in France, was assassinated, and as France slid into anarchy the alliance with Wales came to an end. Glyndŵr's own men, who were not professional soldiers, had to return home for long periods to attend to their families, crops and animals. Parts of Ystrad Tywi and Ceredigion were in consequence lost to Owain.

In the opinion that Owain's career was coming to an end, in 1408 the English hastened to Wales from all parts of their country, hoping to be in at the kill. The sixth royal invasion, in which England's naval superiority was more obvious than ever, was led by the English prince of Wales who would become Henry V. They brought large cannons and other engines of war from distant parts of England to accomplish their main objective, which was to capture the castles of Harlech and Aberystwyth. Rhys Ddu repelled a heavy attack on Aberystwyth before it was finally taken. When Harlech was captured in 1409, Owain's wife Marged, two daughters and three grand-daughters were taken prisoner to London.

English authority was still endangered in many parts of Wales by Owain's guerrilla activities. His last battle was fought near his home ground in 1410. Rhys Ddu, Philip Scudamore and Rhys ap Tudur were taken prisoner and executed as traitors to England. In 1411 Maredudd ap Tudor, great-grandfather of Henry VII, and two of his half-brothers, all close relations of Glyndŵr, were executed for their part in the war of liberation. Glyndŵr himself took to the mountains with groups of 'Owain's children' as his followers were called. He was never finally defeated on the battlefield but was overcome by the attrition made possible by England's huge resources. Nevertheless, sporadic attacks were made by groups under his command for another four years. In 1412 he captured Dafydd Gam, the notable anglophile Breconshire nobleman who had fought on the English side throughout the war. Gam, who was released on the payment of a ransom, died of his wounds at Agincourt after being knighted on the battlefield by Henry V.

For a period after Owain's final disappearance some of his followers lived as outlaws in the mountains. Royal officials failed to traverse Merioneth in 1416 'for fear of the Welsh'. Maredudd ab Owain, one of Glyndŵr's courageous sons, continued his resistance with substantial help from Gwynedd until 1421. He even tried to raise a rebellion there with the help of the Scots.

On the mainland of Europe, where Owain had won recognition for Wales, there were moves in her interest as late as 1415, eleven years after the French treaty was signed. In that year Gruffudd Young, Glyndŵr's chancellor, was present at the Conference of Constance. There the English delegation maintained that the Welsh were a part of the English nation. Prompted by Gruffudd Young the French delegation successfully contested this, maintaining that Welsh nationhood was distinct from the English. Thus Wales was first proclaimed a nation in

Europe by the French.

Nothing is known of Glyndŵr after 1415. Possibly he ended his days in the home of the Scudamore family into which his daughter Alys had married, in the Welsh-speaking part of Herefordshire. Despite the huge temptation to betray him, his people were loyal to the last. Just as there had been no challenge to his leadership, there was no hint of betrayal. Mystery surrounds his death and his grave. Many poets had sung his praise but none sang his elegy. Was he still alive? 'The majority,' said a Welsh chronicler, 'say that he died, the soothsayers say he did not.'

Welsh Confidence Remains

Despite the appalling destruction and poverty caused by half a generation of war, and despite the racial malice of the penal legislation imposed on the Welsh people, and even on the English husbands of Welsh wives, by England's parliament, the stronger confidence and deeper patriotism bequeathed by Owain Glyndŵr were evident. Gruffydd ap Nicolas of Dinefwr, grandson of Henry Don with whom Glyndŵr had corresponded at the outset of his campaign, illustrates this. Though not the most admirable character, the last thing that could be said about him was that he was servile to the English government. For instance, when he was summoned to Westminster to answer for the wild behaviour of his son Thomas, not only did he refuse to go but when commissioners were sent to investigate the situation they received short shrift, says Ralph Griffiths. 'Intimidated by a display of armed retainers, benumbed by judiciously applied liquor and flayed in open court by an indignant Gruffydd, they were arrested and sent back to

London humiliated and wearing his livery.' The son of the aforesaid wild Thomas, Sir Rhys ap Thomas, was the most powerful man in Wales after the considerable contribution he made to Henry Tudor's victory on Bosworth field. Gruffydd led the Lancastrians until he was supplanted by Jaspar Tudor, uncle of Henry VII.

Gruffydd was a cultured and sincere Welshman. His close friendship with Humphrey Duke of Gloucester attests to this. Humphrey, who was one of the chief architects of the Renaissance in these islands, spent much time in Wales as Justice of the Principality. Gruffydd's most valuable cultural contribution was made as patron and president of the famous 1453 eisteddfod, one of the most important in Welsh history, for it was at this eisteddfod that the twenty-four metres of Welsh prosody were agreed. The chair was won by Dafydd ap Edmwnd, one of the greatest poets of the Great Century, as the fifteenth century is known in Welsh literature. The flowering of Welsh poetry itself attests to the deep confidence of the Welsh people. The eisteddfod was probably held in Carmarthen castle which Gruffydd had made his home, and on which he had dared to spend in 1452 the largest sum of royal money spent on any of the king's buildings in southern Wales since Glyndŵr's war of liberation.

The bards had sung the praises not only of Owain Glyndŵr and his men but also those of 'Owain's Children' who continued to fight after his day as outlaws in the mountains and forests. Some, such as Dafydd ap Siencyn, were well-known. Like Owain himself, Dafydd was a relative of the Tudors. A *cywydd* of praise to him by the famous Tudur Aled opens with this couplet:

> Dy gastell ydyw'r gelli,
> Derw dôl yw dy dyrau di.

> *Your castle is the woodland,*
> *The meadow oaks your towers.*

Occasionally a bard himself became an outlaw. One of the greatest poets, Lewys Glyn Cothi, was an example. He thanked Owain, the son of Gruffydd ap Nicolas, for his protection when he was in that position:

> A mi'n nhiredd Gwynedd gynt
> Yn herwa, yno hirhynt,
> Owain i gadw fy einioes
> Ei aur a'i win im a roes.

> *Once when I was in Gwynedd's lands*
> *a long while with outlaw bands,*
> *to preserve my life, Owain*
> *gave me of his gold and wine.*

It is strange that a saga similar to the Robin Hood stories did not gather around these patriotic brigands.

Despite the confident pride and delight of the Welsh people in their cultural heritage, the half century after Glyndŵr saw the beginning of the process which led to the servitude and ruin of Cymru the nation. Ironically, this was due to what was perceived as a success. Behind the Welsh attitude to the coming revolutionary change in the way Wales was governed lay the ancient myth that Ynys Prydain (The Isle of Britain) had been, and would again be, governed by the Britons under a British king in London. It was Nennius in the ninth century who wrote in his book on Welsh history that the day would come when the Britons would again be in possession of the island. The belief lingered on, colouring Welsh thought and action, until recent centuries. It was Welshmen in London, significantly, who established in 1751 the first society to study the history and literature of Wales, calling it *Y Cymmrodorion* (The First Inhabitants). And when in 1792 Iolo Morganwg organised a colourful meeting, again in London, to celebrate the ancient literary tradition of Wales, it called itself, and is still called, the Gorsedd of the Bards of the Isle of Britain.

The key to the response of the Welsh military and political events was their search, led by the bards, for a national Deliverer. Owain Lawgoch and Owain Glyndŵr had in the past been expected to be the Deliverer. Now other candidates appeared in the Wars of the Roses which, says Trevelyan, were to a large extent a quarrel between Welsh lords who were also great English nobles closely related to the crown. For both Yorkist and Lancastrian factions Wales was a prolific source of troops, whose leaders were often Welshmen. The bards saw them as fighting in their turn for Welsh national freedom.

The first Yorkist leader was William Herbert of Raglan, in the heart of the eastern Marches where the Yorkists were strongest. Herbert, who became earl of Pembroke, was a notably generous patron of bards and harpists and was said to be more fluent in Welsh than in English. A grandson of the Dafydd Gam who was knighted on the field of Agincourt, he himself won fame as a soldier. He had fought in Normandy with the heroic Mathau Goch, a nephew of Glyndŵr's wife. After his victory at the battle of Towton he was made Justice of southern Wales and was given the task of winning the whole of Wales over to the Yorkist cause. Guto'r Glyn called on him to unite Wales and free it from English rule:

Na âd arglwydd swydd i Sais
Na'i bardwn i un bwrdais;
Barna'n iawn, brenin ein iaith
Bwrw yn tân ein braint unwaith …
Dwg Forgannwg a Gwynedd,
Gwna'n un o Gonwy i Nedd.

My lord, don't give the English office
Nor pardon to a burgess;
King of our language, be aware
Their rights were once thrown in the fire …
Bring Glamorgan and Gwynedd,
Make one from Conwy to Nedd.

The bards rejoiced at Herbert's military victories and at his political success as chief adviser to the king, failing to see that Welsh nationalism was being used for party ends, not for the last time. He was enthusiastically proclaimed the nation's leader. For the bards the wars were fought for Welsh national issues, not English dynastic ones.

William Herbert's glory did not last long. The battle of Banbury was the last he fought. In that bloody encounter thousands of Welshmen were killed, including a hundred and sixty eight prominent members of the aristocracy and squirearchy. William Herbert was captured and executed. The bards saw this as a terrible blow to Wales, for:

Gwinllan fu Raglan i'r iaith.
Raglan was our tongue's vineyard.

Another notable Welshman who was killed at Banbury was Tomas ap Rhosier, Herbert's half-brother, whose home, called Hergest, was in Welsh-speaking west Herefordshire. He too was a generous patron of the bards, but is best-known as the keeper of *Llyfr Coch Hergest* (The Red Book of Hergest), one of the most splendid collections of Welsh manuscripts.

Deeply involved in the Wars of the Roses, but on the Lancastrian side, were the Tudors of Penmynydd, Anglesey, cousins of Owain Glyndŵr, who fought gallantly for his cause. It was to this family that the bards now looked for a Deliverer who would be the saviour of Wales.

The Fateful Battle of Bosworth Field

Owain ap Maredudd ap Tudur, who had been a page boy to Henry V when twelve years of age, had fought for the king in France. On his return to England he dropped Maredudd from his name and adopted Tudor as his surname and Owen as his Christian name. While bathing naked, the enterprising Owen was spotted by Catherine de Valois, Henry V's young widow. They were secretly married. When she met her monoglot relations-in-law she found them 'the goodliest dumb creatures she ever saw'. Henry VI made his Tudor half-brother's sons, Edmund and Jasper, earls of Richmond and Pembroke. The earl of Richmond married the remarkable Margaret Beaufort when she was thirteen years old. She gave birth to a boy two months after Richmond's death in Carmarthen where he was buried in the House of the Greyfriars. The boy, Henry, was taken by his uncle Jasper to Pembroke castle where he lived for fourteen years. Some of his life was conducted in the Welsh language. But after William Herbert's victories Jasper and Henry fled from Wales to Brittany where he was for years kept under house arrest by the Duke of Brittany. After William Herbert's execution at Banbury the poets' support swung to Henry Tudor.

Herbert's death left Wales leaderless. The establishment of the Council of the Principality, which had been invested in the prince of Wales, improved the situation but the Council came to an end when the prince became king, and the administration deteriorated again. Largely for this reason Henry Tudor was to march through Wales with an army of 4,000 men, mainly French, which had landed in Milford Haven without any resistance at all. There was no enthusiastic welcome either. He was not joined by a force of a thousand Welshmen from Ystrad Tywi, under the command of Sir Rhys ap Thomas, until he reached the north-eastern English border. About a third of the army which won the battle of Bosworth and the English crown for Henry Tudor was composed of Welshmen.

A Pyrrhic Victory for the Welsh

The battle of Bosworth, as Trevelyan said, set upon the throne of England the greatest of all her royal lines. The Welsh hopes of centuries could be said to have been fulfilled. In the eyes of the bards, a man of Welsh descent on the English throne in London fulfilled an ancient prophecy. Robin Ddu had sung:

> Y mae hiraeth am Harri,
> Y mae gobaith i'n hiaith ni.
>
> *For Henry there is longing,*
> *And there is hope for our tongue.*

'To the Welsh people,' said Bacon, 'Henry's victory was theirs; they had thereby regained their freedom.' In addressing the leaders Henry Tudor himself had spoken of his determination to 'restore the said Principality of Wales and the people of the same to their former liberties'. However that should be understood, one way was stated by the Viennese ambassador: 'For the Welsh it can now be said that they had won back their old independence.' This factor, and still more the increasing freedom of the gentry to build their estates, go far to account for the lack of opposition to English rule that had been indigenous throughout the past. Its quiet acceptance was further promoted because England enlarged her power and influence in Wales without undue oppression. Although Wales the nation paid the price of national subordination, individual Welshmen prospered as never before. No longer regarded as scrubs, they were given an honoured place in London society and the royal court. Some, like the Cecils, even became rulers of England.

Throughout this relaxed period great poets continued to sing and great scholars to labour, almost wholly in the Welsh language. 'For two centuries,' said Anthony Conran, 'Wales had enjoyed an outburst of fine poetry, unrivalled for its sophistication, its brilliance and poise, by anything the Celts have ever achieved, before or since. Poet after poet, many of them of a standard one must call great, attained to a classical elegance in their art that English poetry can only match in the later years of Elizabeth and the seventeenth century.'

For Ever and Henceforth Incorporated and Annexed

The grim national cost of personal prosperity was paid during the reign of Henry Tudor's son. His chief minister Cromwell proudly declared, 'This realm [England] is an empire.' Every aspect of the menial status of the Welsh nation demonstrated Cymru to be a colony. This was made starkly clear by the words of the 1536 Act of Incorporation which was passed by the English parliament four years after Celtic Brittany was incorporated in France. The Act is commonly called the Act of Union, but the union was that of Jonah and the whale. There is a non-scriptural tradition that the whale spoke to Jonah. 'Now Jonah,' it said, 'we two are one. And I am that one.' So was it in the Act of 'union' between England and Wales. The two states certainly became one, but England was that one.

The Act of Incorporation declared, 'That this said country or dominion of Wales shall be, stand and continue for ever henceforth incorporated, united and annexed to and with this Realm of England.'

The Marcher Lordships were abolished and local government was based on thirteen counties subject to the English parliament. One of the counties, Monmouthshire, was placed in the Oxford circuit, giving rise to the title 'Wales and Monmouthshire,' which continued until Plaid Cymru's Carmarthen by-election victory in 1966.

Welsh law was completely abolished. 'The Act of Union offered no compromise,' said Hywel Emanuel; 'English law "and none other" was to apply throughout Wales.' Welsh law was among 'the sinister Usages and Customs' differing from England which were to be 'utterly extirped'.

The fundamental purpose of the Act was to merge Wales in England, to assimilate the Welsh, to destroy their separate national identity. Where there were two nations there was to be one, and England was that one. In this it differed fundamentally from the 1707 Union of England and Scotland. The Scotish nation was not assimilated by England. It surrendered its state to the English state.

However, the purpose of assimilating the Welsh could not be achieved as long as the Welsh spoke a different language from the English. It was the language above all else which had maintained a sense of nationhood in Wales. Lacking any national political structure, Wales the nation would have disappeared if the language were lost. That was a fate devoutly wished by English government, which despised it as, in the words of the Act, 'a speeche nothing like, nor consonant to, the natural Mother Tongue used within this realm'. As Edmund Spenser had said, 'It hath been the use of the conqueror to despise the language of the conquered.' The Welsh gentry of the 17th and 18th centuries and many of the middle classes of the 19th and 20th centuries, allied themselves with the English conqueror.

The most dangerous clauses in the Act of Incorporation were those concerning the language. The seventeenth clause lists a number of legal and political officials who must proclaim and hold all the sundry courts of the land in the English tongue and all oaths etc; 'and also from henceforth no person or persons that use Welsh speech or language shall have or enjoy any manner office or fees within this realm of England, Wales or other the king's Dominions upon pain of forfeiting the same offices or fees, unless he or they use and exercise the English speech or tongue.' If a justice of the peace spoke Welsh in the course of his duties he was dismissed.

Thus did Cymru become a totally powerless region in the highly centralised English state which dominated and exploited it instead of serving it in a subordinate position as a state should, destroying rather than strengthening the fabric of its national life.

Welsh Self-confidence Fades

A lamentable consequence of the battle of Bosworth and the Act of Incorporation was to weaken and almost extinguish the splendid confidence and will to live which had characterised the *Cymry* for a thousand years. Within a few generations of the Act most of the aristocracy and squirearchy, from which a nation's leaders were normally drawn, were anglicised. When the natural leaders lost their sense of national loyalty, national morale was bound to be debilitated. Engrossed by personal ambition, the upper classes failed to produce a single national political leader. They allowed their nation to wilt and decay.

Within a quarter of a century of the Act of Incorporation Gruffudd Hiraethog, the last of the great medieval poets, noted the odious psychological weakness that now afflicted his fellow-countrymen who had left their country for England. After a short while away from home, he said, they deliberately forgot the language of their native land. A few years later the great scholar Siôn Dafydd Rhys made the same point, writing in Italy where he was the chaplain of the famous Cardinal Borromeo. Although we may speak English, French, Italian or some other language, he said, some of us affect an ignorance of our own language. In the same year Morris Kyffin, an upper-class literary man and a soldier of note, accused prominent churchmen and a host of others of despising the language of their country and of being ashamed to speak it or hear it lest their status should suffer.

Aristocrats and Squirearchy Turn their Backs on their Nation

By the end of the seventeenth century most of the aristocrats and squirearchy, who had been the patrons of Welsh culture, had renounced not only the national tongue but the nation itself. The English people, soon to be called British, whose ignorance of Welsh culture was absolute, regarded the Welsh language as a jargon beneath contempt. A seventeenth century author wrote:

> The native gibberish is usually prattled thoughout the whole of Taphydom except in their Market Towns, whose inhabitants being a little rais'd, and (as it were pufft up into Bubbles) above the ordinary Scum, do begin to despise it. 'Tis usually cashier'd out of Gentlemen's Houses ... so that (if the stars prove lucky) there may be some glimmering hopes that the British language may be quite extinct and may be English'd out of Wales.

Although Wales suffered next to no physical oppression, the endless psychological violence which exploited the growing Welsh sense of inferiority imperilled both the language and the nationhood of Wales. Yet Dr R.M. Jones points out that if the Welsh had retained their backbone and had resisted English political oppression with the vigour of the Irish, English oppression might have been even more ruinous in Wales than in Ireland.

The dangers were mitigated by a substantial group of able humanists who strove hard for the language as cultural nationalists. When the bardic order, though not the poetic tradition, was coming to an end for lack of patronage, they produced splendid prose works, grammars and volumes of history. Most of them were committed Protestants, though they included such Roman Catholics as Siôn Dafydd Rhys referred to above. Some of them, such as Bishop Richard Davies and the great William Salesbury, propagated the theory of the existence in the distant past of an apostolic Celtic Church independent of Rome. This influential theory promoted Welsh national dignity. The renaissance in scholarship which bore fruit in a number of classics made a valuable contribution. But the outstanding masterpiece was the translation of the Bible into magnificent Welsh by Bishop William Morgan. It is not too much to say that the Welsh Bible, published in 1588, was the salvation of the Welsh language. Christianity has been a powerful formative influence throughout the history of Wales. But for its power, the nation's life and language would have been unlikely to survive to modern centuries.

The translated Welsh Bible, 1588

The Struggle of the Cultural Nationalists

The enervating Welsh lack of confidence would obstruct the fight for the conditions of a full national life throughout the ensuing centuries. It was possible for Hussey Vivian, the wealthy squire of Penllergaer, to state in 1863 in a National Eisteddfod address referring to the English and the Welsh, 'At this time we are one whole compact people. Remember that you are all Englishmen though you are Welshmen … depend upon it, we must consider ourselves Englishmen.' That was a typical – if comic – example of the thought of the thousands among whom the success of the Act of Incorporation had been limitless. It illustrates the truth that the fundamental responsibility for the political and psychological oppression of the British state in Wales has been that of the Welsh people themselves. Will, not force, is the basis of the state. If the people of Wales had not willed government by an English and then a so-called British state, that government would have ceased to exist in Wales.

Despite the serf mentality of so many of the upper and bourgeois classes, Wales was not lifeless. Though there was no struggle for national freedom, a palpable minority took pride in the language and literature, music and history of Wales. In striving for these aspects of the nation's life they indicated a will to live. A vitally important aspect of the literary renaissance which began in the last quarter of the sixteenth century was the number of historical works published. Its history is a nation's memory. A knowledge of its past cannot fail to strengthen emotional attachment to the nation and so deepen national consciousness. Although much of the history propagated was mythical, it nevertheless fostered a sense of national identity. In particular the attempts of scholars in England as well as in Wales to prove that Geoffrey of Monmouth's *History of the Kings of Britain* was the literal truth, nurtured Welsh pride. In the eighteenth century the history and literary traditions of Wales were effectively promoted by London Welsh institutions such as the Honourable Society of the Cymmrodorion and the Gwyneddigion.

A Literate Nation

The growing literacy in the Welsh language was notably enhanced by the remarkable circulating schools organised throughout Wales by Griffith Jones, vicar of Llanddowror, Carmarthenshire, with the help of Sir John Phillipps whose sister he married. About half the population of Wales attended these schools where they learnt to read the classical Welsh of the Bible. Their influence spread outside Wales. In 1764 a report on them was commissioned by Catherine, empress of Russia. In the next generation hundreds of thousands of people of all ages were taught to read the Bible in Sunday schools organised initially by Thomas Charles, an Oxford graduate from Carmarthen.

Griffith Jones said that the purpose of his circulating schools was not to make gentlemen, but Christians. He furthered this aim also as a powerful preacher who addressed large congregations in the south-west. In fact he was a precursor of the dynamic spiritual awakening which exploded in the middle of the century under the leadership of men in their early twenties. Calvinistic in doctrine and Welsh in language, the revival transformed the life of the Welsh people between the mid-eighteenth and the mid-nineteenth centuries. The thousands of chapels built by an impoverished but serious-minded people were the centres not only of their religious life but of a rich social and cultural life as well. Usually there was some activity in the chapel buildings every night of the week, except perhaps on Saturday, though there were often special preaching or musical festivals on Saturday night as well. In the *Cymanfa Ganu* (Singing Festival) the influence of one of the three main leaders of the mid-eighteenth century revival was perpetuated in the hymns of William Williams, known as Pantycelyn, the name of his farm. A profound psychologist, he had a deep interest in science. According to Saunders Lewis, 'He is the great discoverer of the unconscious, the stronghold of the passions, and he is the first poet of science and the modern mind in Europe.' Many of Pantycelyn's thousand hymns are beautiful lyrics:

William Williams

> Rwy'n edrych dros y bryniau pell
> > Amdanat bob yr awr:
> Tyrd, fy anwylyd, mae'n hwyrhau,
> > A'm haul bron mynd i lawr.
> *I look across the distant hills*
> > *Each hour for thy coming:*
> *Come, my loved one, for it's late*
> > *And my sun's near to setting.*

Melysach nag yw'r diliau mêl
    Yw munud o'th fwynhau,
Ac nid oes gennyf bleser sydd
    Ond hynny yn parhau.

Sweeter than the honey drops
    A minute's joy in thee,
And I've no other pleasure that
    Lasts everlastingly.

A phan y syrthio sêr y nen
    Fel ffigys îr i'r llawr,
Bydd fy niddanwch heb ddim trai
    Oll yn fy Arglwydd mawr.

And when the stars of heaven fall
    Like ripe figs to the sword,
There'll be no ebb to the delight
    That's all in my great Lord.

With very few exceptions, the leaders and artists of Wales in all fields now sprang from the *gwerin* (the people – a combination of the working class and lower middle class). A notable product of the cultured Nonconformist gwerin of the mid-nineteenth century was Daniel Owen, the finest of the Welsh-language novelists. Born and bred in Welsh-speaking and industrial Mold within a few miles of the English border, he made his living as a tailor. His father and two brothers were colliers and all three were killed in the Argoed pit when water flooded their shaft. Daniel's father had an excellent voice and the would-be rescuers could hear the father and the sons singing a hymn in which the others joined. As the water level rose the voices of the doomed men weakened minute by minute until the silence was total.

At this time heavy industry had been developing for three-quarters of a century. Far from destroying the Welsh language it strengthened its hold. The reason was the direction taken by rural emigration. Whereas migrants from rural Ireland and Scotland had gone mainly to England, the United States and other overseas countries, Welsh migrants moved mainly to Welsh industrial areas, taking their language, customs and values with them. For instance, in 1830, Merthyr Tydfil, which was one of the biggest industrial towns in the world, was almost wholly Welsh-speaking. Iron-workers, colliers and their families packed the dozens of Welsh-language Nonconformist chapels. The town became the major centre of Welsh cultural life.

But Merthyr Tydfil was also the locale of an astonishing struggle for social justice. It was far from being a placid town. Among the eighty thousand who lived in the vicinity there were thousands who enjoyed gambling, heavy drinking, boxing and racing. The taverns were the meeting places of the poets and of a variety of cultural and humanitarian societies, which included the Ivorites and Oddfellows, the Cymreigyddion and Cymrodorion, Gomerians and Brythoniaid, the Llenyddion Merthyr (Merthyr Literati) and the Rhyddymofynwyr (The Freethinkers), a political society, all conducted in the Welsh language.

It was as the main centre of Welsh radicalism that Merthyr Tydfil led the struggle for social justice. Dr Gwyn Alf Williams described how the social convulsion began with a mass rally on the hills above the town. The raising of the red flag, for the first time in the countries of Britain, indicated that the fight for social justice was on, under the leadership of Lewis Lewis, known as Lewsyn yr Heliwr (the Huntsman). Thousands marched to the town, besieged the magistrates in the Castle Hotel, destroyed a Debtors' Court, restored to their owners goods which had been seized by the Court officials, forced a strike at the ironworks and called the men of Monmouthshire to join the rebellion. The rising became what Dr John Davies calls 'the most ferocious and bloody event in the history of industrial Britain'.

Eighty Argyll Highlanders marched from Brecon barracks to restore order. They were posted at the Castle Inn. The workers attacked them in a frontal assault. At least twenty-four civilians were killed and seventy injured. Nevertheless, the military were driven from the town.

Merthyr Tydfil was in the hands of the workers for four days. The professional soldiers and yeomanry sent from Swansea were defeated twice. The workers yielded only when faced with the levelled muskets of four hundred and fifty troops who were brought to Merthyr to prevent thousands of Monmouthshire workers from reaching the town, and afterwards a further eight hundred professional soldiers converged on the district.

Two men were condemned to death – Lewsyn yr Heliwr and Dic Penderyn, a twenty-three year old miner. Lewsyn's sentence was commuted to exile for life in Australia, but Dic, who was innocent of the crime of which he was accused, was hanged in Cardiff. The last words he cried on the gallows were, 'O Arglwydd, dyma gamwedd!' – 'O Lord, what an injustice!' Thousands followed his body to its burial in Aberafan, thirty-five miles away. Years later a Welshman in the United States confessed to the crime for which Dic was hanged.

The Chartist 'Silurian Republic'

At the end of the decade the spectre of revolution again faced the government, this time among the Chartist workers of Monmouthsire, almost all of them Welsh-speaking. Sir Thomas Phillips, the able mayor of Newport, said that, 'The insurrection of 1839 was Welsh in its origin and character, and carried on with more secrecy because contrived by persons who communicated with each other in a language not understood by the authorities.'

The most significant of their actions was a march on Newport by five thousand men of the coalfields, including five to six hundred armed with guns. They stormed the Westgate Hotel where a detachment of soldiers was stationed. At least twenty Chartists were killed and many wounded. This was followed by the last mass treason trial in the countries of Britain. A hundred and twenty-five prisoners were brought to trial. Three of the leaders were sentenced to be hanged. An executioner came to the town and a scaffold was erected, but a tremendous campaign organised by the Chartists throughout the state of Britain achieved sudden success. The sentence of death was commuted to penal servitude in Australia.

Some historians believe that the aim of the Chartists was to create a workers' republic, called by Harri Webb 'The Silurian Republic', in south-eastern Wales where the Silurians were led against the Roman invaders by Caradog over eighteen hundred years earlier. Ivor Wilkes has contended that industrialisation had produced the first serious challenge to English dominion in Wales since the fifteenth century. The Welsh national element was certainly not absent. Dr William Price, one of the ablest if most eccentric of the Chartist leaders – after the rising he escaped to

France dressed as a woman – called on the Chartists to strike with all their power, remembering that, 'We are the descendants of valiant Welshmen and we must be worthy of the traditions they have passed on to us.'

The Children of Rebecca

Concurrently with the sensational events in industrial Monmouthshire, rural Carmarthenshire seethed with social drama. Carmarthen town was, like Merthyr Tydfil, a centre of radicalism. Chartism flourished there under the leadership of the solicitor Hugh Williams, a brother-in-law of the radical Richard Cobden. His deep convictions were evinced by his defence, free of charge, of the Chartists who had seized the mid-Wales wool town of Llanidloes and held it for a week until they were expelled by the military. He performed a similar service several times elsewhere.

Hugh Williams was the outstanding leader of the Children of Rebecca which attacked, early in the year of the Chartist march on Newport, the first of the one hundred and forty tollgates they destroyed. The numerous tollgates were a harsh oppression suffered by a growing rural population often desperately impoverished. When a new tollgate was installed at Efail-wen on the Carmarthenshire-Pembrokeshire border, Rebecca sounded her bugle and a group of horsemen gathered to lead a host which followed on foot. All wore bonnets, were dressed in women's clothing and had blackened faces. Their title had a scriptural origin: 'and thy seed shall possess the gate of his enemies'. The abuse of power by the landlords, stewards and bureaucrats, usually alien, excited bitter hatred in all parts of the country. In northern

The Rebecca Riots

Wales more than half the land was owned by four per cent of the people. The new Poor Law was a common source of extreme misery, especially the abominable regimes in the workhouses which separated wives from husbands. Many popular ballads drew attention to this inhuman practice:

> Hyd angau, medd y ffeirad ffraeth,
> > Cysylltaf chwi â'ch gilydd.
> Nage, myn diawl, medd Shoni bach –
> > Ond hyd y wyrcws newydd.

> *Till death, says the smooth-tongued priest,*
> > *I join you heart to heart.*
> *Not so, by damn, says Johnny bach –*
> > *'Till the workhouse do you part.*

South-west Wales became ungovernable. After the destruction of the Carmarthen workhouse a force of eighteen hundred troops was drafted in to arrest the miscreants, who proved elusive however. Five thousand people, with four hundred horsemen at their head, marched through the town, to be dispelled by a cavalry charge by the mounted Dragoons, the last cavalry charge in the United Kingdom.

The five Rebecca leaders exiled to Van Diemen's Land included Shoni Sgubor Fawr, the tough red-headed giant of a fist-fighter, and Dai'r Cantwr, the best-known of Welsh ballad singers. The convulsion's Welsh national dimension appeared in rhymes and ballads such as Liberty's Address to the Welsh, published in Carmarthen in April 1839:

> Sons of Cambria! – come, arise
> And no longer be
> Serfs enslaved, whom all despise.
>
> Will ye always bow so meek
> To the imperious nod
> Of a haughty race who seek
> To rule you by the rod!

The activities of Rebecca's Children were not in vain. The government responded with positive action in a number of the causes of discontent.

The alien bureaucracy and the anglicised middle and upper classes were of course appalled by the series of revolts by the spirited industrial and rural *gwerin*. They attributed much of the responsibility for them to the Welsh language. William Williams, the Carmarthenshire-born MP for Coventry, urged the government to inquire into the teaching of English in Wales, saying, 'If only the Welsh had the same advantage for education as the Scotch [sic] they would, instead of appearing as a distinct people, in no respect differ from the English.' To abolish the Welsh 'as a distinct people' was of course the policy of the Act of Incorporation. It was the policy more successfully imposed in Ireland by what Padraig Pearse called 'the murder machine'.

'The Treason of the Blue Books'

Despite the absence of Welsh national political institutions, and despite her extremely vulnerable geographical situation, the Act of Incorporation failed to assimilate Wales. It remained a distinct nation. It was the astonishing survival of the ancient tongue as the language of a rich Welsh civilisation that made this possible. The situation was utterly transformed by the enormous growth in the power of the hostile centralist English state and the in-migration of many hundreds of thousands. The state should serve the nation in a subordinate position, strengthening every aspect of the nation's life. So, far from strengthening the language and culture of Cymru, the British state devitalised them.

The attitude of the state was exposed by the infamous report of the Commission set up to make a case for English-only education. The authors of the 1852 report were three monoglot Englishmen who were totally ignorant of Welsh-speaking Nonconformist Wales. They shared the opinion expressed by William Williams MP when he called in parliament for the Commission: 'A band of effective schoolmasters is kept up at much less expense than a body of police or soldiery.' Only a third of those interviewed were Nonconformists. The great majority were clerics in the Church of England, many of them bitterly

The Treason of the Blue Books

hostile to Nonconformity and the Welsh language. The Report's fundamental conclusion was that 'The Welsh language is a vast drawback to Wales, and a manifold barrier to the moral progress and commercial prospects of the people. It is not easy to overcome its evil effects.' Its opinion of Nonconformists was equally hostile, while it found the sexual morals of the Welsh women to be uniquely lax. Some clergymen alleged that the chapels were responsible for the immorality.

Although a significant minority in the episcopal Church enthusiastically supported the national tongue and enriched Welsh literature and culture, the consequences of what became known as *Brad y Llyfrau Gleision* (The Treason of the Blue Books) were many and complicated. The established church became known as *Yr Estrones* (The Stranger). Its disestablishment became the prime radical aim and led to the combination of the long tradition of cultural nationalism with political nationalism.

The invigoration of cultural nationalism among the *gwerin* is illustrated by the birth of the Welsh national anthem. The author and composer of the anthem, *Mae hen wlad fy nhadau* (The old land of my fathers), worked together, father and son, as weavers in Pontypridd where the Rhondda river runs into the Taff. It was in 1856 that Evan James, the father, went for a walk along the banks of the Rhondda river to consider a letter he had received from his brother inviting Evan to join him in the USA. He put into verse his reasons for feeling unable to leave his homeland. On returning home he wrote them on paper. They were simple verses which sang of the poets and musicians of the old country *(yr hen wlad)* and the patriotic warriors who fought in its defence. The closing line affirms that it was for freedom that they shed their blood. In the second verse he celebrated Cymru's mountainous beauty, every valley and crag, every river and stream, and the sea as a rampart for the beloved land. Then the opening hammer blows of the chorus drive home the poet's loyalty to his land and his passionate will that its language shall live for ever. James, the twenty-four year old harpist son of the poet, was deeply moved by his father's verses. That evening he took the same path along the River Rhondda's bank and on his return sang the poem to the tune he had newly composed. It quickly became popular and for nearly a century and a half it has been recognised as Cymru's national anthem. How fitting that it should have been written and composed by two of the cultivated *gwerin* at a time when Pontypridd was almost a hundred per cent Welsh-speaking.

Michael D. Jones

While the Treason of the Blue Books made the majority of Welsh people more anxious to please the English people, and deepened their servility in matters Welsh, it had the reverse effect on a significant minority. One such was Michael D. Jones, considered by many to be the greatest Welshman of the century. Born in Llanuwchllyn, Merioneth, in 1822, it was in the USA that Michael D. Jones was awakened to the fact of Welsh nationhood by the angry response to the Treason of the Blue Books in one of the sixty Welsh-American periodicals published in the United States during the century. At the time he was the young minister in an Independent Welsh-language chapel in Cincinnati, the capital of Ohio, whose governor was Michael D. Jones's brother-in-law, Welsh-speaking William Bebb. He returned home a formidable patriot, a radical Nonconformist nationalist who saw no consistency in standing for personal freedom but against national freedom. The nation was for him the human community to which its members should give their political, social and cultural loyalty. Loyalty is the heart of Welsh nationalism.

The Treason of the Blue Books taught Michael D. Jones that the main obstacle which impeded the growth of a Welsh freedom movement was servility. Therefore he concentrated his energies on striving to restore national confidence and self-respect. As it was glaringly obvious to him that the huge English majority in the parliament of England made the concept of a Welsh democracy bogus, he called for a Welsh parliament and for an independent Welsh national party to achieve it. The establishment's policy of trying to create one British nation on the territory of the British state obviously involved the dissolution of the nations of Ireland, Scotland and Wales in an essentially English nation. Clearly the abolition of the Celtic languages was intended to further that end.

Michael D. Jones

Michael D. Jones merged his political and his cultural nationalism into one comprehensive policy. That combination of two strands of nationalism has characterised Welsh nationalism ever since. It has always believed that the cultural entity and the political entity should be one. Together with R.J. Derfel, who called in 1864 for a national university, library and museum as well as a Welsh government, Michael D. Jones initiated and fostered the modern Welsh nationalist movement. In accord with the convictions of Michael D. Jones, the Plaid Cymru of recent generations has been non-violent and internationalist.

The Patagonian Venture

The most remarkable of Michael D. Jones's ventures was the colony he founded in Patagonia. The mid-nineteenth century was a time of heavy migration from the growing population of rural Wales. Fortunately, the great majority of the migrants went to the steelworks and mines of the valleys of south-eastern Wales, but tens of thousands went overseas, especially to the USA which had seen several attempts from the seventeenth century onwards to establish Welsh-speaking communities. Michael D. Jones himself had plans for settlement in the States, not because he favoured migration. He was facing the fact that unless the people streaming out of Wales were organised in strong communities they would quickly lose their Welsh language and values.

Eventually a promise of a tract of land in empty Patagonia, and that in time the area settled by the Welsh should be recognised as an Argentinian state, drew a few thousand to a Welsh-language settlement far from English influence. The first 163 people, mostly from the southern coalfield, sailed in the *Mimosa* for *Y Wladfa*, as the settlement was called, on 25 May 1865, and landed in Porth Madryn on 28 July. *Y Wladfa* can claim to be the first independent Welsh political action since the Act of Incorporation.

At the outset the difficulties were appalling, especially the cruel drought which was ably overcome by a system of irrigation. The settlers were hit by tragedies, one particularly bizarre when Llwyd ab Iwan, Michael D. Jones's son, was murdered on the pampas by bandits, perhaps Butch Cassidy and the Sundance Kid.

Yet when Michael Jones visited *Y Wladfa* in 1870 he found that the settlers had overcome the enormous difficulties to establish a very different order from the one they had left in the homeland. He could report that they were practising his policies. In Wales he had roundly denounced capitalism and the greed for wealth which corrupted the lives of capitalists, but he found *Y Wladfa* run as a democratic cooperative order. As he himself wore clothes made of home-spun materials in order to encourage small Welsh industries, so too did the Patagonian Welsh. As he had pressed for home ownership in Wales, so too did each family in *Y Wladfa* own its own home. The colonists had overcome extreme privations triumphantly and had won the warm friendship of the native people. In particular they had mastered the difficult but vitally important skill of irrigating the wilderness.

The most radical difference between the social order of *Y Wladfa* and that of the homeland was in the place given to the native tongue. Whereas in Wales the Welsh language had been expelled from legal and public life by the Act of Incorporation, in the Patagonian colony it was the community's first language for every purpose. The law courts were conducted in Welsh and Welsh was the language of officials and bureaucrats. Whereas in Wales English was the language of education, *Cymraeg* (the Welsh language) was the only medium used in the schools of *Y Wladfa*. The Welsh nation had no kind of governing political institution, and in the English parliament Welsh was treated as a foreign tongue. One was not allowed even to take the oath in Welsh. *Y Wladfa* was governed by an elected Council whose only language was Welsh.

The members of the Council were elected by ballot

whereas in Wales voting was public; farmers could be evicted by their landlords and quarrymen dismissed by quarry owners for voting according to their conscience. In *Y Wladfa* men and women had the right to vote at eighteen years of age, whereas in Wales no women of any age had the right to vote for another two generations, and women and men of eighteen years had to wait a century for the right to vote. *Cymru fach* (little Wales) was governed for a short while, before the intervention of the Argentinian government, in the way Welsh nationalists wished the homeland to be governed. But the Argentinian government prevented the growth of a Welsh democratic state, fearing that it would give Britain the excuse to invade Patagonia as it had invaded the Malvinas a generation earlier.

Michael D. Jones knew that his vision of a Wales both Welsh and free would never be realised without a strong independent Welsh political organisation to concentrate on promoting it. He was a great admirer of the Irish nationalists who had done just that. In conjunction with Emrys ap Iwan, the ablest of his close disciples, he did make an effort to establish a Welsh national party, but organisation was not one of his talents. His inspiration spread, however, and affected some of the most influential people of the period, all of them Nonconformist radicals. Such was O.M. Edwards, the greatest of the cultural nationalists. The son of a Llanuwchllyn crofter he was for decades an Oxford history don who was later knighted for his massive contribution to Welsh education and culture, literature and history. He even found time to publish a popular children's magazine whose editorship was taken over on his death by his son, Sir Ifan ab Owen Edwards, the founder of the amazing youth and children's movement, *Urdd Gobaith Cymru* (The Order of the Hope of Wales). Sir O.M. Edwards spoke many times of Michael D. Jones's inspirational qualities, as when he wrote:

> He aroused my interest in Welsh history and taught me to see the glory of those who had struggled for Wales, while at school I was taught to admire those who had injured her. He kindled my zeal, fired my ambition, set a goal before me ... I got in his company something no school or college ever gave me – an enlightened love of Wales and her history, and an unshakeable belief in the powerful force which has since been given the name Nationalist ... For a year he taught me to write Welsh history from a Welsh standpoint ... In leaving Bodiwan, the old hero's home, I would be determined to do all I could to serve our country and its *gwerin*.

Tom Ellis, Lloyd George and Liberal Domination

Another of Michael D. Jones's disciples who often expressed his debt to him was Tom Ellis, son of a tenant farmer, an Oxford graduate deeply steeped in Welsh culture, who at the age of twenty-seven shattered the squirearchy not only by winning the parliamentary seat of Merioneth but winning it on a wholly Welsh programme, including self-government. Michael D. Jones's influence was heavily reinforced by Parnell and the Irish Nationalist Party, and by the years he, like O.M. Edwards, spent among the young nationalists of the University College of Wales, Aberystwyth. These erased the impact of the very English education given in the contemporary schools, both primary and secondary. A textbook in a Merioneth school at the time of Tom Ellis's youth contained the following gem:

> And all of you ought to remember that the great nation to which you belong, and of which I hope you are all proud, is bigger, far bigger than the two little islands that make up the kingdom of Great Britain and Ireland, and that it extends everywhere where the English language is spoken by men who live under English law and under the English flag … and we owe our good fortune mainly to England being an island … Look at the map at the beginning of this book and think of what is meant by all those red patches … They mean that in every part of the world so marked there are countrymen of ours living and working: that in every continent and in every climate there are men and women who read the same English Bible as we read.

Extreme imperialistic British nationalism of this kind was wholly acceptable to many, perhaps most, members of the growing Welsh middle class such as Talhaiarn, a prosperous architect and popular poet. Although he did not insist, as Hussey Vivian or the author of the textbook quoted above did, that the Welsh were English, he was equally confused about the identity of the Welsh people. For him they were British. 'We now form an integral portion,' he said, 'of the great nation whose flag waves on every sea and in every clime.' For generations the national identity of the Cymry has been weakened by the idea, ardently fostered by the English establishment, that they are members of a phantom nation called British.

The Britishness at the heart of British imperialism was a growing threat to Welsh national identity. It was coupled with the mounting power of the centralist British state which into time became the most centralist in Europe. The English state, into which Wales had been assimilated by the Act of 1536, had been renamed British after the surrender of the Scottish state in 1707, although in fact it was still English. A.J.P. Taylor, the most popular historian of his day, accepted this as the truth. 'Until August 1914,' he wrote, 'a sensible law-abiding Englishman could pass through life and hardly notice the existence of the state ... All this was changed by the impact of the Great War ... the history of the English state and of the English people merged for the first time.' The English people are more than 80% of the people of the United Kingdom of Great Britain and Northern Ireland. The Welsh are 5%.

Britishness was fostered by war from the Napoleonic wars to the world wars of the twentieth century. But apart from geography and the state everything British was English. If the national movement had not survived and grown, the nation of Cymru could have been Britished out of existence. Choirs, rugby and laverbread would not have ensured its future. By the beginning of the twenty-first century, however, Welsh nationality seemed secure. An opinion poll early in the year 2000 indicated that, despite the enormous in-migration of recent decades – a third of the population of Cymru were born outside the land – 82% of her people thought of themselves as Welsh first.

Though Tom Ellis was influenced by British imperialism, he was first and foremost a Welshman. Only a man of Welsh integrity could say that 'The English establishment lies like a dead corpse on the back of the Welsh nation.' Tom Ellis was the finest of the new generation of able Welsh politicians whose nationalism was both political and cultural. He worked extremely hard despite his poor health. When he was on holiday in Egypt in 1889 he was struck down by typhus and diphtheria and brought to the verge of the grave. Even so, after being bedridden for twelve weeks, he wrote on St David's Day of his passionate love of his homeland and set forth his vision of the Wales he longed to see, concluding with these words:

> ... but most importantly of all, let us work for a Legislative Assembly elected by the men *and the women* of Wales, and responsible to them. It will be a symbol and a binding of our national unity, a tool to implement social and industrial ideals.

Though his health was permanently impaired he continued to labour for the land he loved, for which his death in his fortieth year was a sad blow.

The Short-term Development of Political Nationalism

Lloyd George was a third influential disciple of Michael D. Jones, who often spoke with gratitude of his inspiration. It was at a meeting addressed in Blaenau Ffestiniog by Michael Davitt, leader of the Irish land movement who was invited to Wales by Michael D. Jones, that Lloyd George first came into political prominence. On the death of Lloyd George's father, who was born and who died in Pembrokeshire, he and his brothers were taken by their mother to live with their cultured shoemaker uncle in Llanystumdwy, Gwynedd. Like Tom Ellis four years

Lloyd George

earlier Lloyd George won a parliamentary seat, the Caernarfon Boroughs, at twenty-seven years of age with an unapologetic radical and nationalist address. During his first decade in parliament he was a sincere and active Welsh nationalist.

The main political weakness of these able men was their failure to create an independent nationalist party as the Irish had done – but they did establish Cymru Fydd, a short-lived national movement, inside the Liberal Party, which included a parliament for Wales among its aims. This movement grew rapidly after Lloyd George assumed the leadership in 1894. For two years he laboured diligently, addressing meetings in every part of the country, including dozens of places in the coalmining valleys where support was much stronger than in the heavily anglicised towns. Behind his policy was 'the conviction that Wales would be an example to the nations of the world if it were given self-government'.

Hundreds of new branches were formed and the North Wales Liberal Federation was taken over.

The Anglicised Welsh and the English in-migrants of south-east Wales were responsible for its collapse. Cymru Fydd suffered its fatal blow in an attempt – in a Newport meeting in January 1896 – to persuade the South Wales Liberal Federation to amalgamate with it. It was proposed by Elfed, the finest poet of those years and a future archdruid, but when Lloyd George spoke in support he was howled down. The chairman, Alderman Robert Bird, a Cardiff businessman from Bristol, declared: 'Throughout South Wales there are thousands upon thousands of Englishmen ... a cosmopolitan population who will not tolerate the predomination of Welsh ideas.'

The *Western Mail* described the meeting as 'a bear garden'. Lloyd George expressed his anger in *Y Faner*. 'Is the mass of the Welsh nation,' he asked, 'willing to be dominated by a coalition of English capitalists who have come to Wales not to benefit the people but to make their fortune?' From then on Liberal support rapidly declined and disintegrated. Four years after the Newport meeting Cymru Fydd had faded away. Yet one can attribute the creation of a National University of Wales, a National Library and a National Museum to the influence of the cultural-political nationalist activities which were for a few years organised in Cymru Fydd. Ironically, Lloyd George's brilliant success as a London-centred British nationalist politician strengthened Welsh attachment to the London order as Henry Tudor's Bosworth victory had done.

The obvious lesson to be learnt from this first Welsh experience of organised nationalism is that to be effective it must be independent of the English political parties. Cymru Fydd's fatal flaw was its embodiment in the Liberal Party. Welsh national political opinion can be truly effective only when organised in an independent political party. A huge hanging block of granite can be moved by being constantly struck by a small stone on a piece of string because the stone is independent of the rock.

Six years after Cymru Fydd's oblivion the Liberal Party won every parliamentary seat in Wales except for Keir Hardie's in Merthyr Tydfil, and Lloyd George became a splendid Chancellor of the Exchequer. Scores of Liberals obtained offices or honours but only a small handful of individuals, like Llywelyn Williams and E.T. John, worked for Wales. 'When E.T. John rose on 11 March 1914 to present his Self-government for Wales measure,' said Sir Ben Bowen Thomas, 'the few who were there listened to his voice as the cry of one risen from the dead.'

Then came the world war to speed the process of Britishising Cymru out of existence. 280,000 Welshmen, two-thirds of the country's male population between twenty and forty years of age, served in the armed forces, a bigger proportion than in England or Scotland. Absorbed by millions of Englishmen in the military system, they were frequently forbidden to write home in Welsh.

The Labour Party, Believing in Self-government, Takes Over

Liberal domination did not last long. It was soon replaced by the Labour Party whose leader, Keir Hardie the MP for Merthyr Tydfil, was a Celtic Christian Home-ruler. The Liberals' Welsh bequest to him was a powerless peripheral region, but under his leadership and for some years after his death the Independent Labour Party strongly supported self-government for Wales. That explains why so many early members of the Welsh National Party had belonged to the ILP. Hardie had been influenced by his friend Jean Jaurès, the great French socialist leader who was assassinated on the eve of the First World War because he believed like Hardie that a general strike should be called if the government declared war. Jaurès also believed like Hardie that the nation is an invaluable community. 'If you destroy the nation,' he said, 'you will sink back into barbarism.'

The Labour Party's sincere support for Welsh self-government was proved by an uncompromising statement made in 1918 by Arthur Henderson. This was no attempt to collect Welsh votes, for Henderson was Labour's most experienced heavyweight. He had been Labour's representative in Lloyd George's War Cabinet and it was he with the Webbs who had devised Labour Party policy in 1918. He was expected to be Labour's first Prime Minister. The weight behind the following words is therefore hard to exaggerate:

> The Labour Party is pledged to the widest and most generous measure of home rule that can be devised ... We regard the claims of Wales to self-government on these lines as strictly analogous to those of Ireland ... Nationalism means the vigorous development of the material and moral resources of the whole people. It is hardly possible to conceive an area in which a scheme of parliamentary self-government could be established with better chances of success than Wales ... Given self-government Wales might establish itself as a modern utopia, and develop its own institutions, its own arts, its

own culture, its own ideal of democracy in politics, industry and social life as an example and an inspiration to the rest of the world.

This was the language that Plaid Cymru would speak. At no time has it been attached to the 19th century concept of an absolutely sovereign nation state which independence entails. Although the Labour Party had always known that self-government would be good for Wales it soon became antagonistic on concluding that it would not be good for the party.

In the 1922 general election, the last of a series of three, the *Welsh Outlook* declared that no election in living memory had paid so little attention to Welsh affairs. The Labour Party, which formed a minority government, had abandoned the principles and values which had inspired Keir Hardie and Arthur Henderson, while the Liberals had forgotten the policies which Michael D. Jones had urged on Tom Ellis and the young Lloyd George. A final home rule conference held in Shrewsbury in 1922 proved to be a fiasco. Even the fifty people who attended it were at odds with each other. Though cultural nationalism retained some vigour, political nationalism which had been expressed solely through the British parties was moribund. 'By 1922,' says Hywel Davies, 'the distinctiveness of Welsh politics in terms of issues seemed to be at an end.' Not a single concession which recognised the existence of a Welsh nation was made by the London government in the inter-war decades. That position would probably have continued to this day but for the growth of Plaid Cymru, the Party of Wales.

The Formation of Plaid Cymru, The Party of Wales

The fight for national freedom during the last two generations has been led by, almost confined to, Plaid Cymru, The Party of Wales, the first independent Welsh political party committed to the nation of Cymru and to national freedom. It was established in a Pwllheli café during the National Eisteddfod week in 1925 by six men who represented three very small movements. The meeting had been called by H.R. Jones, a former quarryman who was the party secretary until his death five years later when he was followed for thirty years by the indefatigable J.E. Jones. For a year the president was Lewis Valentine, a scholarly Baptist minister who had been dangerously wounded in the horrific Somme battle. He was followed for thirteen years by Saunders Lewis, a brilliant dramatist, novelist, poet, literary critic and political thinker. Many consider Lewis to be the greatest Welshman of the twentieth century. He too had been badly wounded in France.

The tiny party's first task was to survive. It succeeded in this and at the same time awakened in many a consciousness of Welsh nationhood. After two years' work H.R. Jones could report that it had over four hundred members including 65 quarrymen, 50 farmers, 70 students and 25 ministers of religion. Such was the movement that challenged British imperial might in Wales. In a further two years' time it fought in Caernarfon its first parliamentary election, gaining 609 votes, 1.6% of the total. It fought Caernarfon three times before the war, winning 2,534 votes, 6.9 per cent of the total, in the third. It held no local government seats in the party name.

Hywel Davies, the historian of the party's first two decades, concludes that it had proved to be little more than an educational/cultural movement. Of course the circumstances in which it was formed were exceptionally difficult. Wales was sinking into appalling economic depression. Unemployment would reach 38 per cent, the worst in Europe. The native language was in steep decline. Britishness was weakening national consciousness. The three wealthy English parties were deeply entrenched, while the new little party's resources were woefully limited. I attended a special meeting of the party executive in 1938 which was called by Saunders Lewis to decide whether or not the party was to continue. Its crippling debt made it impossible to pay its organiser. The debt was £350!

The Leadership of Saunders Lewis

The party, despite the difficulties it faced, made a deep impression, due in large part to Saunders Lewis's charismatic presidency. He was a very unusual person to say the least. The son of a Presbyterian minister in Birkenhead, he became a Roman Catholic. In a notably pacific party he was an admirer of the military character. Most of his economic, political and cultural policies were fully supported by the members, but his advocacy of a monolingual Wales probably failed to gain majority approval while his plea for the deindustrialisation of southern Wales was thought by most, perhaps, to be totally impossible, although it could be seen as part of a case for sustainable development which the party strongly favoured. Many however considered his medievalism and belief in the need for a cultured aristocracy to be bizarre.

Nevertheless, some of the most bitter criticisms levelled at Saunders Lewis have been totally unjust. For instance, accusations of fascist leanings have been made by his critics for seventy years without proof. The truth is that Saunders Lewis was further from fascism than the Labour and Conservative parties. Unlike those highly centralised parties, which built dominating centralist states, he was a thoroughgoing decentralist who strongly opposed capitalism and centralist socialism and strongly supported the creation of a cooperative order in Wales. Fascism entails an all-powerful centralist state which has absolute sovereignty. Mussolini's slogan was, 'Everything within the state, nothing without the state.' Saunders Lewis rejected the absolute sovereignty entailed by independence. 'Freedom' was his word. He worked for the measure of freedom that would enable the Welsh nation to be herself.

Saunders Lewis

The Variety of Nationalisms

This confusion of Welsh nationalism with fascism, deliberate more often than not, lay behind the bitter opposition to the struggle for Welsh national freedom, a struggle applauded in many other countries. Opponents of Welsh nationalism sought to give the impression that it was a part of an evil blanket of nationalist ideology, despite the obvious fact that there are as many nationalisms as there are countries. The nationalism of Gandhi is different from that of Mandela, and both are very different indeed from Hitler's and Stalin's. The strong and positive nationalisms of the Scandinavian countries, long-time models for Welsh nationalists, are in a different world from the virulent nationalism of Balkan countries. The non-violent, internationalist, decentralist nationalism of Plaid Cymru is obviously unlike the centralist British nationalism which derives from imperialism; its totem is the Trident submarine. The British nationalism of the Anglo-British parties is so secure that their members fail to see themselves as nationalists.

A consequence of Plaid Cymru's renunciation of violence has been its unwavering opposition to nuclear weapons since the Hiroshima bomb was dropped. For years its strong support for CND was shared by such Labour leaders as Neil Kinnock and Robin Cook. They abandoned their principles when their electoral unpopularity hindered Labour's rise to power. They have even supported New Labour's commissioning of a fourth Trident submarine and the investment of a further £100 million to enhance Trident power. Each submarine's 48 warheads is five times as powerful as the bomb that destroyed Hiroshima. The Trident submarines maintained by the New Labour government have the capacity to kill millions of people, each one innocent and each one of infinite value. But Great Britain's great power status, the nationalist object of the excercise, can be said to have been maintained.

Saunders Lewis resigned as President in 1939 and withdrew from political action immediately after the war. Why did he do so? There was more than one reason. When I met him in 1946 on my way to a radio debate with Iorwerth Thomas, the virulently anti-Welsh MP for Rhondda West, Saunders Lewis told me that it was his Roman Catholicism which had forced him to cease political action. His profound influence was due less to his policies than to his inspiring leadership, his tremendous integrity, and a combination of outstanding ability with a gift for public speech and a prodigious dedication to Cymru and the language he loved so passionately.

Welsh Language Programmes' Threat to the English Language

The first major success achieved through Saunders Lewis's leadership was in the field of radio broadcasting in the Welsh language. From the 1920s to the 1950s, radio was as powerful a medium of communication as the press. A Welsh-language radio service was therefore essential to the survival of the national tongue. This view was not shared by the English establishment, whose opposition was a revelation of its contemptuous attitude to Wales the nation, its language and culture. Five years after the establishment of the British [sic] Broadcasting Corporation there were no Welsh or English-language radio programmes broadcast from Wales. The only Welsh-language programmes heard were in a weekly half hour broadcast from Dublin by Radio Eireann. When nationalists demanded a Welsh-language service, the BBC, through E.R. Appleton, director of the Western Region, made the following reply:

> Wales, of its own choice, is a part of the British Commonwealth of Nations, whose official language is English. When His Majesty's Government decided to establish a Corporation for the important task of broadcasting it was natural that the official language should alone be used ...
>
> To use the ancient languages regularly – Welsh, Irish, Gaelic and Manx – would be either to serve propaganda purposes or to disregard the needs of the greatest number in the interests of those who use the languages for aesthetic and sentimental reasons rather than for practical purposes ...
>
> If the extremists, who want to force the Welsh language on the listeners of the region, should get their way, the official language would lose its grip.

In the inter-war years, Wales was for the London government no more than a geographical expression. In 1934, twelve years after its establishment, the BBC renounced even that. Its Western Region, centred on Bristol, included the whole of western Britain to Land's End. 'The Western Regional Station,' declared the BBC with a surpassing knowledge of history, 're-unites the Kingdom of Arthur after years of separation by the Bristol Channel.' The BBC Controller of Programmes stated, 'It is felt that the claims of Wales will thus be adequately met, and I can hold out no hope of any reconsideration.'

Plaid's fight was joined by a committee, which included Saunders Lewis and Lloyd George, set up by the University Court. In the same year a major cause of the BBC's stubbornness was revealed when the new BBC Director for Scotland declared that he was 'in charge of the only Broadcasting Region that was a nation'. Nevertheless, Wales was soon recognised as a national entity and grudgingly permitted three-quarters of an hour daily of Welsh-language programmes, which were completely deleted on the outbreak of war. After a bitter struggle, two ten-minute slots were conceded at poor broadcasting times. There was no slackening in the fight for an independent Welsh broadcasting corporation. After two decades of struggle a federal system was secured in which a Welsh Broadcasting Council was responsible for all programmes originating in Wales. Now both Radio Cymru and Radio Wales have a splendid service for eighteen hours a day each.

The Fire in Llŷn

Plaid Cymru was put on the map by the dramatic fracas caused by the government's decision in 1935 to place a 'bombing school' in the heart of the Welsh-speaking Llŷn peninsula. Led by Saunders Lewis, the opposition was based on two grounds. One was its purpose, to train men in the techniques of bombing military and civilian targets from the air; the other was its location in a wholly Welsh-speaking area of historic importance. It would turn one of the essential homes of Welsh culture, idiom and literature into a site for the promotion of a barbarous method of warfare. The government had intended establishing similar institutions in Northumberland and Dorset but refrained in both places, in the north because historians protested that historic Lindisfarne would be harmfully affected, and in the south because of the proximity of a swannery. But in Wales, despite the protests of organisations representing some half a million people, it went ahead. The Prime Minister refused to meet a deputation of national leaders. A letter signed by tens of prominent Welshmen was sent to *The Times*. It was rejected. This was wholly consonant with the arrogant attitude of the British establishment towards Wales in the inter-war decades.

In consequence, after ensuring that no one would be injured, a group of Welshmen took action. As a symbolic act of protest they set fire to the bombing school's stacks of timber and building materials. Three of them gave themselves up to the police. The three were Saunders Lewis, Plaid Cymru's president; Lewis Valentine, the party's first president and first parliamentary election candidate; and D.J. Williams, a 'character' of extraordinary gaiety and purity of heart whose books will be read as long as the Welsh language is read, a farm-worker and then for ten years a collier before proceeding to the universities of Wales and Oxford.

In the trial at Caernarfon, Saunders Lewis gave one of the most impressive addresses ever heard in a court of law. It was almost wholly in English as the defendants were not allowed to address the court in Welsh.

The jury failed to agree on a verdict. The case was then transferred to the Old Bailey so that the defendants could be tried by their equals. They were sentenced to nine months' imprisonment. After spending their sentence in Wormwood Scrubs prison they were welcomed home to Wales by a gathering

of fifteen thousand people in Caernarfon's huge pavilion. But Saunders Lewis was sacked from his post as a lecturer at the University College, Swansea.

The Influence of D.J. and Noëlle Davies

Personal loyalty to Saunders Lewis was strengthened by his sacrificial heroism, but probably more influence on party policy and organisation was carried by Dr D.J. Davies, a colourful character who had experienced in school the humiliating 'Welsh Not' which entailed punishment for speaking Welsh. At twelve years of age he became a miner. After working in a number of pits he went to the USA, visiting every state but one. A successful boxer, he fought some forty bouts. He worked in mines from Pennsylvania to Colorado and was nearly killed by a fall of tons of rock. He was convinced that he would not have survived but for his healthy lifestyle. He studied law in a university until his money ran out. He became a trade union organiser and was dismissed more than once as an agitator. His experience of the ruthless methods of coalowners made him a Marxist socialist. He joined a party of surveyors whose work took him to Alaska, the Yukon, China and Japan.

In May 1918 D.J. joined the American navy as an Engineer Class 1, where his boxing prowess made him a welterweight champion. When in the following December his ship struck a mine he was among the minority who survived after spending days in an open boat in the North Sea. He left the American navy in July 1919 and returned home to work in a mine. A serious accident two years later prevented him from working for three years and he left the mines for ever in 1924.

He threw himself into activity for the Labour Party during his five years at home, but he abandoned Marxism to embrace a humane cooperative socialism. Although he accepted class as a basic fact of social life, he no longer fought for class but for community. He saw his socialism as 'a harmonious system of society where spiritual values take preference over material values'. D.J.'s values were very different from those of the majority of South Wales socialists for whom a statement made by Iorwerth Thomas, MP for Rhondda West, in a radio debate with me was more typical: 'The stomach has superseded the conscience.' And Neil Kinnock's declaration on his class allegiance in a Parliamentary debate on devolution was a more accurate, if confused, reflection of Welsh Labour's attitude to class than was D.J. Davies's. Neil Kinnock said, unapologetically:

> I believe that the emancipation of the class which I have
> come to this House to represent can be best achieved in a
> single nation and a single economic unit, by which I
> mean a unit where we can have a brotherhood of all
> nations ...

The most important turning point in D.J. Davies's life was his stay, after leaving the mines, at the Danish International College in Elsinore. Peter Maniche, the Principal, said that he was the best male student he had known in his long period in the post. There he met a young Irish woman, Noëlle French, whose academic career in the National University in Dublin had been extraordinarily brilliant; she won four first class honours. She fell in love with this humorous Welsh miner, and so began a partnership unique in Welsh politics.

Davies became a lecturer in a folk college. While there he experienced a spiritual conversion to which Noëlle no doubt contributed, though it was advice given to him by the college principal, Gronwald Nielsen, which proved crucial. 'Your country,' he said, 'is ruled by England. Your duty, young man, is plain. You must go back to Wales and work to make her free.' D.J. protested that there was no hope of success; England was so strong and Wales so weak. He never forgot Nielsen's answer:

> The path of duty is plain before you and you must tread
> that path. That is the important thing for a human being
> – not whether you succeed or fail, but to do what is
> morally right.

D.J. Davies returned to Wales and joined Plaid Cymru, on whose policies he afterwards had a profound influence. He was the author of Plaid's decentralist community socialist policy, and it was he who persuaded the party to adopt dominion status as its constitutional aim – the party has never been attached to the 19th century model of absolutely sovereign nation states. Plaid Cymru's constitutional policy was outlined in the 1960 Conference. It entailed entering a confederal order with England in which there would be no tariffs, tolls or passports between the two countries, but there would be a common external tariff. A uniform tax system and a common commercial policy would further unite the two countries. Standing ministerial conferences, a permanent secretariat and an investment bank would be necessary. Under this order Wales would not have the absolute sovereignty of independence. The aim of the party has always been national freedom. It was D.J. Davies who induced it to move its central office, indeed its only office, from Caernarfon to the southern anglicised city of Cardiff, and to make greater use of the English language, including the publication, in addition to its Welsh monthly, of an English monthly periodical and numerous English pamphlets. Saunders Lewis, who had concentrated on the salvation of the Welsh language, was influenced by him even on the language issue, as well as on many others. In a letter written to D.J. Davies in 1931 he said:

> About the language matter. Do you feel that our members are fanatical about it? I agree that they don't study other aspects of nationalism enough, and that they lack an embracing synthesis in which language and literature have a place and no more and no less, but that is due to the one-sided tradition of Welsh culture, its lop-sided development. But especially among our young people I feel there is a growing appreciation of your point of view, and a broader conception of nationalism so that I hope you'll soon find them coming round to you.

Fighting for the National Language

D.J. Davies was fully in accord with the consensus view of Plaid Cymru that the future of the Welsh nation depended on the survival of the Welsh language, which therefore had to be given a place of priority among the party's policies. Many in the Labour and Liberal parties, or in no party at all, shared this opinion. Therefore they sympathised with Plaid's major pre-war activity, which was to organise a parliamentary petition calling for official status for the national language. Although four hundred thousand signatures had been collected before the war terminated the campaign, the government made no response. Nor would the government have taken any action but for the pressure brought by Undeb Cymru Fydd, the non-party pressure group, and Plaid Cymru when the War Office seized 65,000 acres on the Epynt Mountain and evicted sixty-two families, moving the Welsh language border some ten miles to the west.

Two of the evicted farmers found farms in Llanddeusant, the next parish to Llangadog where I then lived. Two years later they were 'brought before their betters', as the unhappy Welsh idiom has it, in the Llangadog village court, for failing to plough enough land. They asked permission of the members of the court to give their evidence in Welsh. This was granted and the person who usually acted as interpreter, a conductor of the splendid local choir and a former signalman on the line in Llangadog, was called for. Then the clerk of the court told the defendants to pay him on their way out.

I was stunned, not realising that this was a normal practice in Welsh-speaking Wales. My experience had been almost confined to large ports in Glamorgan where Arabs, Greeks and other non-English-speaking seamen were frequently brought before the courts. Their evidence had to be translated, of course, but the court would never dream of asking them to pay the interpreter. That would be the grossest injustice. Only Welsh people had to pay to speak their native tongue in a Welsh court of law.

The matter was raised in the Undeb Cymru Fydd Council. In consequence the Welsh Parliamentary Party agreed to send a deputation of six to Cardiff to meet six members of Undeb Cymru Fydd. The result of the meeting was The Welsh Courts Act. All that this feeble Act did was to permit non-English-speaking Welsh people to give evidence in Welsh in a court of law in Wales without paying for the privilege. The over half a million Welsh people whose first language was Welsh, but who could speak English, were still compelled to speak English in a Welsh court of law.

Welsh Nationalism Here to Stay

It was widely expected by opponents of Plaid Cymru, and feared by its supporters, that another world war would see the end of the national party and even of the nation itself. The people of the countries of Britain would throw themselves wholly into the defence of England and the British state in such massive numbers, as they did in the First World War, that few would be left to defend Wales. It was hoped that Plaid Cymru would fulfil that function under the presidency of J.E. Daniel, an able and committed academic, after 1939. It is not surprising that it alone of the political parties strove to defend Welsh national life and that no other party made an attempt to keep the issue of national freedom in the public eye. Although still no more than a political pressure group, it emerged from six years of war stronger than it entered. Whereas it could fight only one seat in the last pre-war general election, it fought nine parliamentary seats, including two by-elections, in 1945. And its political activity increased outside the electoral field.

Defending Welsh Land

Plaid's long struggle in defence of Welsh territory and Welsh-speaking communities won considerable sympathy in Wales. The War Office alone possessed 500,940 acres of Welsh land, three times the amount held in Scotland which is four times the geographical area of Wales, and fifteen times as much as the War Office held in Northern Ireland which is a little smaller than Wales. On occasion direct action was taken to defend the land, which was usually farmed by a Welsh-speaking community. Such was the case in Trawsfynydd when the War Office tried to add ten thousand acres to the thousands already in the hands of the military camp there. For two days the roads to the camp were blocked by Plaid members, preventing lorries, vans or cars entering or leaving.

Most of the land struggles were successful, reducing land held by the War Office by over two-thirds. Similar success was achieved by Plaid Cymru in land struggles against the Electricity Commission and the Forestry Commission which had outrageous plans to plant a million and a quarter acres of Welsh land.

Campaign for a Welsh Parliament

Although a few members of the Labour and Liberal Parties, including five Welsh Labour MPs, supported the Campaign for a Welsh Parliament, not one of the three Welsh Liberal MPs appeared once on its platform. The grinding work of collecting signatures on a parliamentary petition calling for a Parliament for

Wales was done almost wholly by members of Plaid Cymru, and Elwyn Roberts's incomparable organising talents were put by the national party at the disposal of the Campaign. In addition the Campaign had in its President, Lady Megan Lloyd George, a star attraction in the scores of meetings addressed by her throughout the coalmining valleys and all parts of urban and rural Wales. Dai Francis, the popular miners' leader, was also a supporter. The petition presented to parliament by Goronwy Roberts MP contained nearly a quarter of a million signatures. Once again there was no government response, but in the 1955 election Plaid Cymru gained a respectable average of four thousand votes in the eleven seats it fought.

The handful of Labour MPs who supported the Campaign for a Welsh Parliament were bitterly reprimanded for doing so, for the Labour Party was overwhelmingly opposed on the local and the British level, as I discovered during a quarter of a century on the Labour-controlled Carmarthenshire County Council. It even withdrew its membership of the Welsh Association of Local Authorities because of its national Welsh character. It was amazing how far their anti-Welshness would go. The party was content with a third-rate negligible nation.

Planned explosions were numerous at this time, mainly against targets connected with the exploitation of Welsh water resources. The British political parties never failed to charge non-violent Plaid Cymru with responsibility for them. They immediately did so when an explosion in the Pembre airfield seriously injured an airforce officer. George Thomas, the Welsh Secretary of State, time and time again accused the nationalists of the dastardly act, repeating the charge when he came especially to Carmarthen to visit the injured man in hospital. The police knew the charge to be untrue. I had received two letters from a vicar in the English midlands who, though without sympathy for Welsh nationalism, was disturbed that innocents were charged with the crime. He gave detailed information which indicated that one of his parishioners, who had taken a post in the Pembre airfield four days previously, was responsible. When I showed the police the letters, they said they were well aware of the facts. Yet no charge was made against the man responsible, who had been sent to the mental wing of an RAF hospital before moving to Australia. Nevertheless, George Thomas continued to accuse nationalists of the crime. There were also at this time notorious examples of the use of *agents provocateurs.*

Two amusing incidents illustrate Labour's attitude to the language and nationhood of Wales. I had been invited by the Worker's Education Authority to give a lecture on Welsh history in a summer school to be held in council premises in Ferryside. The council's Labour leader rose to break this dangerous news to the council. On behalf of the Labour caucus he declared that the WEA summer school would not be held in council premises unless the request that I lecture on Welsh history was withdrawn. The WEA refused to withdraw. The summer school, had to be held in other, less suitable, premises.

On another occasion I had succeeded in persuading the council to experiment in simultaneous translation of speeches made in the Welsh language. Although nearly all the Labour members were Welsh-speaking, not one of them spoke a word of Welsh in the debate. I alone did so. When the cost of the simultaneous translation system was given, an appalled Labour member jumped to his feet and cried, 'For that sum we could have a new urinal in Blue Street in Betws!'

Labour's attitude towards the language and nationhood of Wales extended to the party's higher reaches. For instance, Welsh Labour MPs campaigned energetically against the establishment of Welsh-medium schools. When George Brown was the Labour Chancellor of the Exchequer in the 1960s he famously declared in Gwynedd that 'The price of a pound of beef is more important than your bloody language.' The Labour Party from the early 1920s to the early 1990s was a centralist British nationalist class party. With individual exceptions it regarded the concept of a Welsh state as wicked. For nine years Neil Kinnock typified the party's attitude as its leader.

The attitude of the Communist Party in Wales was totally different. Under the leadership of its organiser Idris Cox, who had been the editor of the *Daily Worker*, it published a substantial pamphlet arguing for a Welsh united front, and another pamphlet in the following year, 1945, calling for a strong series of devolutionary measures and sturdy support for the Welsh language.

Defending the Tryweryn Valley

In the second half of the 1950s, Plaid Cymru was mainly responsible for organising its biggest campaign hitherto. This was in defence of the land and community of the Tryweryn Valley and the village of Capel Celyn in Merioneth against Liverpool's threat to drown the valley. The village postmaster of the richly cultured community was Watcyn of Meirion whose daughter Elisabeth was the splendid secretary of the Defence Committee. Another daughter was seven times a winner in the National Eisteddfod, while Watcyn himself was a noted singer, poet and choirmaster. The opposition of the people to drowning their homes was unanimous and utterly resolute. With the sole exception of a twelve-months old child they all marched with banners in protest through the streets of the huge alien city of Liverpool, and then made the long journey to Manchester where they made a most impressive programme on Granada Television in the early days of the medium.

A host of public meetings were held throughout Wales and two, each attended by hundreds, in Liverpool and one packed meeting in the House of Commons. A mass rally was held on the banks of the Tryweryn river. 1,055 public bodies, including a hundred and twenty-five local authorities, declared their opposition. When the Liverpool measure came before the House of Commons the only Welsh MP to support Liverpool bore two great Welsh names, David Llywelyn. Welsh opposition to drowning the Tryweryn Valley and destroying its cultured Welsh language community was virtually unanimous. But there was no Welsh democracy. The united Welsh opposition was overwhelmed by the huge English majority in the Parliament of England which had incorporated Wales over four centuries earlier.

Nevertheless, the nationalist campaign had a considerable effect on the government. When it became clear that Welsh nationalism was here to stay and that it threatened to continue to grow, the government began to make concessions. Although they were very small they were significant, for they indicated that – unlike its attitude in the pre-war decades – the government acknowledged the existence of a Welsh nation.

First came a Welsh Day in Parliament, then in 1946 the first annual White Paper on Welsh Affairs. A Welsh Regional Council for Labour was established in 1947 and a Council for

Labour, chaired by Huw T. Edwards, in 1948 to advise the government on Welsh affairs. Next, the Tories appointed a Minister for Welsh Affairs attached to the Home Office, and then a Minister of State was appointed to assist him. Cardiff was recognised by the Tories as the capital of Wales and an office was set up there to superintend the economy. The Welsh Grand Committee was set up in Westminster.

These minor concessions reflected the growth of Plaid Cymru in the fifteen post-war years. But although its support was bigger at the end of the war than at its beginning, it was still very small. When I was elected to the Carmarthenshire county council in 1949 I was the only member of Plaid Cymru on a county council in the party name, and Wynne Samuel was the only nationalist on a district council in the party name. By the end of the 1950s, and the end of the Tryweryn campaign, however, Plaid Cymru had a number of members on local councils in the party name. Although the growth of Plaid Cymru was slow in the first two post-war decades it was, despite Scotland's enormous advantages over Wales, greater than the growth of the SNP. One advantage was that the Labour Party was not as dominant in Scotland as it was in Wales. In the 1950 election the Tories got 50% of the Scottish vote. Labour has never achieved that. In 1959 it fought twenty of the thirty-six parliamentary seats, whereas the Scottish National Party, despite the huge advantages it enjoyed, could fight only five of the seventy-one Scottish seats. Plaid Cymru was the stronger of the two parties in the 1950s. Both parties were held back by the power of Britishness.

In 1959 the threat posed by nationalism persuaded the government to site the Llanwern steelworks in Wales rather than in Scotland where it had been expected to be placed. In 1959 too

Plaid Cymru's first parliamentary victory, 1966

Huw T. Edwards resigned from the Chair of the Council of Wales because of the constant rejection of its advice by the government. He joined Plaid Cymru. And in 1959 the Labour Party decided to appoint a Secretary of State for Wales when it came to power. That occurred, together with the establishment of the Welsh Office, in 1964.

Cymdeithas yr Iaith Gymraeg (The Welsh Language Society) formed in 1962 would become a most important wing of the national movement, which had also been strengthened by a number of other societies and organisations including a private company such as Sain which has been so active in promoting Welsh popular music of all kinds.

Plaid Cymru won a significant legal and political victory when it took the Carmarthenshire county council to the High Court for refusing to accept Welsh-language nomination forms in the 1962 county elections. Not only did the success in the High Court lead to the general use of bilingual election forms in the future, but it was also followed by the establishment of the Sir David Hughes Parry committee to advise on the status of the language. As a result of the committee's advocacy of equal validity, the Welsh Language Act was passed in 1967, the year after the Carmarthen by-election.

It was in 1964 that I fought my home constituency of Carmarthen for the first time. Although my vote was a record for Plaid Cymru the deposit was lost; it needed an eighth of the total vote to keep the deposit in those days. The Liberals were 9,700 ahead and Labour was 16,000 ahead. In the next general election eighteen months later on 31 March 1966 Plaid's vote improved, but Labour and Liberal were still far ahead, Liberal by 4,572 and Labour by 13,865. Two months later came the sad news of the death of Lady Megan Lloyd George, the Labour member. A by-election followed on 14 July 1966 which we like to remember was the date of the fall of the Bastille and within two days of the date of Tom Ellis's election for Merioneth a hundred years before, 16 July 1886. Inspired by the Carmarthen victory, Harri Webb wrote one of his rousing ballads:

> When Gwynfor got in for Carmarthen,
> Old Merlin was roused by our roar,
> And we sang the National Anthem
> As it's never been sung before.
>
> In the Square before the Guildhall
> We gathered two thousand strong,
> And as far as Abergwili
> They could hear the triumphal song.
>
> And around us were the thousands
> Of patriots near and far

Who had played their part in the battle
When Gwynfor got in for Shir Gâr.

The Lord Rhys rode with Rebecca,
And Princess Gwenllïan came
At the head of a host of heroes
Long fallen without a name.

There was singing in Pantycelyn,
And a prayer at Blaenycoed,
For we'd learnt from Llanddowror the lesson
That freedom can't be destroyed.

Tryweryn flowed into the Tywi,
And Clywedog flood came down
To burst the dams of betrayal
That night in Carmarthen town.

And the snarling ranks of treason
Slunk away with many a curse
In the dawn of right and reason
As they clambered aboard their hearse.

When Gwynfor got in for Carmarthen
The summer night was sweet,
The breeze blew in from the hayfields
And the people danced in the street.

The transformation of the Welsh political situation initiated by the Carmarthen by-election in a constituency one-third industrial continued in two further by-elections, to the great distress of the Labour Party, in wholly industrial valley constituencies. In Rhondda West in 1967 Vic Davies, the Plaid candidate, reduced the Labour majority from 16,888 to 2,306, and in Caerffili in 1968 Dr Phil Williams brought Labour's majority down from

21,148 to 1,874. The Carmarthen and the Rhondda by-election results probably contributed to inspiring the Scottish National Party and Winnie Ewing its candidate to win their notable victory in Hamilton in November 1967. The by-elections certainly prompted the Rt. Hon. James Griffiths to express his fear that Plaid Cymru could displace Labour as the biggest party in Wales.

The Labour Party had therefore to find a way of defusing the nationalist threat. It acted in two ways. The first was mainly the work of George Thomas, later Lord Tonypandy, whose work as Secretary of State for Wales was marked, said *Planet*, by 'awful provincial shabbiness'. It was a jamboree which exploited the power of the emotional appeal which the English crown and royal family then had. The investiture of the Prince of Wales in Caernarfon castle in 1969 was a hugely successful public relations exercise seen on the television screen by hundreds of millions throughout the world. Dafydd Iwan's brilliant satirical ballads strengthened the militant opponents, but the costly six-week trial of the Free Wales Army – timed to end on the day of the investiture – did serious harm to the wholly non-violent Plaid Cymru.

The second method of defusing nationalism was the time-honoured tactic of appointing a Royal Commission. No doubt the immediate purpose of the Commission, under the chairmanship of Lord Crowther, was to buy time in the hope that the Welsh and Scots freedom movements would go away. Its establishment, however, was a remarkable tribute to Plaid Cymru. For the first time since the 1890s Welsh autonomy was taken seriously by the London government. Crowther, himself a professional economist, praised Plaid's economic plan, which was constructed by Dafydd

Jubilant Plaid Cymru supporters controlled by a good-natured police force

Wigley and Dr Phil Williams. After agonising gestation, the Labour Party gave evidence in favour of an elected assembly, similar to that for which Gwilym Prys Davies had worked so hard, though it would have no legislative powers. The Conservative Party, which was not threatened by Plaid Cymru, declined to give evidence at all.

Although I lost the Carmarthen seat, and Winnie Ewing lost Hamilton, in 1970, Plaid Cymru fought every seat in Wales for the first time in that election, increasing its total vote from 60,000 in 1966 to 170,106 votes, 12.5% of the total. In addition it won a number of local government seats. Those of the English parties who thought once again that nationalism was finished in Wales and in Scotland were disabused when Emrys Roberts won 37% of the vote in a 1972 Merthyr Tydfil by-election, and by Margo Macdonald's astounding victory in Govan, Glasgow.

When the Royal Commission, now chaired by Lord Kilbrandon, published its Report in 1973, the Labour Party had been replaced by the Conservatives as the governing party and no further action was taken. There were two general elections in 1974, both of which were won by Labour, and both of which saw an improvement in the Welsh and Scots nationalist position. On 28 February Dafydd Wigley and Dafydd Elis Thomas were elected as Members of Parliament for Plaid Cymru while I lost at Carmarthen by three votes. On 10 October I was elected, giving Plaid Cymru three seats, while eleven SNP members were elected in Scotland. There were more Scots and Welsh nationalists than Liberals in the Westminster parliament. Two years later Plaid Cymru shook the land by winning control, under Emrys Roberts's leadership, of the borough council of Merthyr Tydfil from where Keir Hardie had led the Labour Party. It also became the biggest party, and formed an administration, on the Caerffili council. Similarly in Scotland the SNP won an impressive number of seats on local authorities.

Stumbling Towards Self-government in Scotland and Wales

The Labour Party could not ignore the growing threat posed in the mid-1970s by the freedom movements in Wales and Scotland, but a half-hearted party with a half-hearted Prime Minister had to face not only the unanimous opposition of the Conservative Party but also sabotage on the devolution issue within its own divided ranks. In the twenty-nine days of parliamentary debates on the Welsh bill, Neil Kinnock and Leo Abse led the open opposition to their government's policy quite unhindered. They behaved as a party within a party, tightly organised, with Donald Coleman and Ifor Davies acting as whips. In the referendum campaign during the winter of snow storms and social strife the Labour opposition, reinforced by the great majority of Labour councillors, effectively deepened the almost limitless ignorance of what the small measure of decentralisation entailed in democratising the bureaucratic government.

What began as a promising advance ended in catastrophe. While Labour councillors stayed at home near the fire, Plaid Cymru members trudged through the snow to deliver Labour leaflets, giving the impression that the exercise was a Plaid stunt. The result was a vote of 956,330 against the assembly and a humiliating 243,048 for it. No wonder Dai Francis, the miners' leader no less, accused the Labour Party of organised sabotage. If it were asked who gained most personally from the perfidy, the answer would probably have to be Neil Kinnock. He would have been unlikely to become leader of the Labour Party but for the ability he displayed leading the destruction of the decentralist measure.

Dafydd Wigley and Dafydd Elis Thomas retained their seats in 1979 but Carmarthen was lost again and there was a decline in Plaid's votes in the industrial south-east. A clear indication of the vital importance of the nationalist vote was that the Conservative government, convinced that nationalist power was now at an end, reneged on its promise to establish a Welsh-language television channel. Cymdeithas yr Iaith Gymraeg (The Welsh Language Society) had waged a heroic ten-year struggle, with Plaid Cymru support, to win this promise from both major parties. The Labour government had begun to implement it. The calamitous referendum vote, the poor general election showing and now in addition the Tory government's abrogation of its

A Cymdeithas yr Iaith demonstration for a Welsh Language Act in central London, 1993

promise of a Welsh-language television service combined to reduce nationalist morale. But few abandoned the struggle. Nevertheless, hundreds, under the leadership of Peter Hughes Griffiths, refused to pay their television licence fees and announced their readiness to go to prison rather than pay. Then on 6 May I announced my intention of employing the Gandhian tactic of continuing on hunger strike, starting on 6 October, until the government kept its promise.

The Language Society renewed its costly campaign, still under the leadership of men and women of extraordinary commitment, and Plaid Cymru wholeheartedly threw itself into the struggle once again. This time it was more of a head-on fight between Plaid Cymru and Mrs Thatcher who had proclaimed herself as 'not for turning'. Three of its most distinguished members, Dr Pennar Davies, Ned Thomas and Dr Meredydd

Evans, had already taken courageous action by forcefully extinguishing the power at the television mast on the Pencarreg Mountain. The first of Plaid Cymru's major actions was the two-thousand strong rally in the Sophia Gardens hall in Cardiff. A series of others followed. Peter Hughes Griffiths could announce at the beginning of September that two thousand had refused to pay their television fees. Michael Foot, who was fully supportive, discussed the matter with William Whitelaw in the middle of September without the presence of civil servants, but his report to me was not too hopeful. A deputation including Dr Gwilym O. Williams, the Archbishop of Wales, Lord Cledwyn, the second Secretary of State for Wales, and Sir Goronwy Daniel, first head of the Welsh Office, also met Whitelaw on behalf of the National Eisteddfod. They too were unable to express hope that the government's broadcasting policy would change. Meantime the story was given sympathetic coverage in the London and overseas press, including a supportive leading article in Welsh in the *Sunday Times*. Television programmes were broadcast on the issue in at least six overseas countries. On 17 September William Whitelaw, twelve months after declaring that the government would not keep its promise, announced that the promise would be kept.

It has kept its word honourably. Eighteen hours a day are now broadcast in the Welsh language on S4C by an independent Welsh institution, evincing the Welsh talent for organisation and increasing the people's self-confidence and strengthening the hold of the national language. What is sorely needed now is an adequate English-language service.

New Leadership in Difficult Circumstances

In 1981 Plaid Cymru was more than fortunate to find a person of such ability and commitment as Dafydd Wigley to become president. He was a man of wide experience to whom I was personally indebted when I was alone in parliament. With Dr Phil Williams and Eurfyl ap Gwilym he was the party's main policy maker. He had successfully held highly responsible economic posts and in Merthyr Tydfil he and Elinor his wife had been pioneer members of the borough council.

But for Plaid Cymru it was a time of growing difficulty. The Thatcherite government, as centralist as Labour had been, was antagonistic to Wales; unemployment was rising steeply and in-migration was increasing by scores of thousands a year, anglicising a host of Welsh-speaking communities and weakening national consciousness all over the land. Electorally, Plaid Cymru suffered from the Labour Party attraction to the protest vote and the attraction of all British parties' growing British imperialist nationalism seen in the Falklands War and the Trident submarine, the evil weapon which is a badge of British nationalism rather than a weapon of military defence. Ever since the first nuclear bomb was dropped on Hiroshima, Plaid Cymru has been an anti-nuclear party.

E.P. Thompson, the historian and anti-nuclear movement leader, said, 'Plaid Cymru today is one of the most internationalist sections of our peace movement'. Thompson recognised that independence was not the Party's aim. The clarity and consistency of the party's leadership on the issue was most impressive.

There were domestic issues on which it also fought without

let. A long-standing example was the exploitation of the rich Welsh water resources. Powerful English conurbations took vast quantities of Welsh water without paying a penny in return. When the Welsh freedom movement demanded payment it was accused of gross immorality. Was not water God's free gift to mankind? Years later, God's gift was privatised and thousands made fortunes selling and buying water. Under pressure from the three Plaid Cymru MPs the Labour government yielded the principle. The Welsh Water Board was paid a very modest £3 million. Even this was too great a measure of justice for Wales for the Tories to stomach. They cancelled it. To add bitter insult to injury the Welsh people had to pay more for Welsh water than the people of Birmingham and Liverpool did.

Plaid's difficulties were increased in the 1980s by the establishment of the Social Democratic Party, which within two elections gained 23% of the Welsh vote. Nevertheless, its position in Caernarfon and Meirionnydd was consolidated and it was strengthened in 1983 in Ynys Môn where Ieuan Wyn Jones came a strong second despite the heavy inward migration. A third of Ynys Môn's population, as of that of Meirionnydd Nant Conwy and Ceredigion, have migrated from England.

Plaid Cymru's ability to hold its own on the parliamentary level, together with its gradual increase in power on the local level, was an indication of its slowly increasing strength, for parliamentary elections had for two decades been fought on television, especially the news bulletins. Not only had Plaid Cymru been denied time to present its programme in party broadcasts, it was also completely excluded from news bulletins. It was literally not in the picture. This was not the responsibility of the BBC or ITN but rather of the major English political parties. Although they denied its existence they held a meeting of party leaders before the election – I attended one – to decide on the allocation of time. In these circumstances of news famine it was no mean feat for Plaid Cymru to hold its own and to grow a little.

Awakening the National Consciousness

To the dismay of the party, tragic family reasons compelled Dafydd Wigley to resign the presidency in 1984. For seven years he was succeeded by Dafydd Elis Thomas, an academic of scintillating talent, whose leadership of the National Left indicated his political bent. He strengthened the tendency of the party which had been described in 1970 by Professor Raymond Williams, who joined the party later, as a part of the New Left. Dafydd Êl, as he was called, was also an active European at a time when members of the party habitually called themselves Welsh Europeans. Dafydd Êl quickly involved Plaid Cymru in the miners' year-long strike in defence of their communities. Throughout Wales, north and south, the party actively helped the miners while Dafydd Êl himself became known as 'the miners' MP', unlike Neil Kinnock who did not put in an appearance for eleven months. Another indication of the nature of Plaid Cymru's politics was its leadership of the opposition to the iniquitous Poll Tax. Plaid Cymru's position was to the left of the Labour Party.

Success in the basic political fight for national freedom depends to a very high degree on awakening a sense of national identity. To strengthen this has been a fundamental aim of the party throughout its existence. Every struggle by the party during the last two generations has added a little to Welsh national

Plaid Cymru MPs, 1987

consciousness. During the last generation the rise of a splendid
school of historians had made a signally important contribution by
awakening the nation's memory.

   An amazing consequence of the national awakening in
many heavily anglicised areas is that scores of thousands of non-
Welsh-speaking parents have sent their children to Welsh-
medium schools, which began to open immediately after the war.
In the Welsh-medium schools of south-eastern Wales, which are
steadily increasing in number, it is usual for 96-98% of the
children to come from non-Welsh-speaking homes. A higher
proportion of children are educated through the medium of Welsh
in Pontypridd and the Rhondda today than in Aberystwyth and
Carmarthen. Their attraction is partly academic. A government

report published early in 1999 revealed that the comprehensive schools of Wales are superior to those of England, and that in Wales the Welsh-medium schools are superior to the English-medium schools. A welcome consequence is that the proportion of Welsh-speaking children, which had been declining for two centuries, is now increasing.

The disheartening aspect of the situation is that the massive in-migration of the 1980s, and to a lesser extent of the 1990s, transformed scores of Welsh-language communities into English-language communities, although the injury has been tempered by the encouraging number of incomers who have identified themselves with Welsh life. In addition, thousands of homes were withdrawn from the local market for young Welsh people by their conversion into holiday homes. The desperate response of some Welshmen who remain unknown was to burn over two hundred such holiday homes. While in-migration adds interest to the developing Welsh national community, combined by outward migration, it is the reason for the uncertain future of the Welsh language.

Cynog Dafis, one of the party's most acute and creative thinkers, who had framed Cymdeithas yr Iaith's manifesto in 1972, produced Plaid Cymru's positive in-migration policy. In conjunction with Dr Phil Williams, Cynog was also involved in developing Plaid's influential Green policy. In the famous National Assembly election of 1999 he chaired Plaid's policy committee.

In 1987 Plaid Cymru won a vitally important victory in Ynys Môn where Ieuan Wyn Jones, who has done so much to strengthen the party's organisation, defeated the Tory candidate.

Two victories made the year 1992 notable in the history of the freedom movement. One was Elfyn Llwyd's success in replacing Dafydd Elis Thomas as the member for Merioneth, with an increased majority. The other was the stunning defeat of the Liberal member for Ceredigion by Cynog Dafis, who leapt to victory from fourth place in the previous election.

The Conservative Party was becoming increasingly bureaucratic. At the end of the Thatcherite period the number nominated by the Secretary of State for Wales to the powerful bureaucratic quangos exceeded the total number of elected councillors. The last four Secretaries of State for Wales – who held the enormous powers of a colonialist governor-general, including a budget of £7 billion – were all Englishmen, without any connection with Wales or any knowledge of Wales when appointed. The Conservative Party in Wales, now known simply as 'the English party', was wiped off the London parliamentary map in the 1997 election. As in the 1906 election, they did not win a single seat in Wales. Although they have governed Wales for three-quarters of the last century they have not once won half the Welsh seats. So much for Welsh democracy.

Plaid Cymru the Second Party, Ahead of Liberals and Tories

The contemptuous attitude of the Tories towards Wales, where unemployment stood at 11% in 1983 and 19% in 1989, was beginning to foster a more decentralist and sympathetic Welsh policy in the Labour Party. The outrageous Conservative treatment of the Language Act contributed to the process. The measure presented by the Welsh Office was lamentably weak. The members of the Welsh Language Board would probably have resigned had not Sir Wyn Roberts, Minister of State, undertaken to strengthen the measure in parliament. However, the amendments were not forthcoming. In order to defeat the amendments proposed by the opposition parties, who held 32 of the 38 seats of the Parliamentary Committee, the Committee was packed by English Tories who raised their eyes from their letter-writing or book-reading only to vote against the amendments.

But a still greater influence on Labour's Welsh policy was Plaid Cymru's growth. In the 1993 county council elections the national party had a bigger number of candidates and won a bigger number of seats than the Conservative and Democratic Liberal parties combined. Although it had only four MPs, that was more than the two oldest British parties had. It was able to declare in 1993 that its youth movement had 1,700 members. The following year its share of the Welsh vote in the European election rose to 17.1%.

Little wonder that the Labour Party felt compelled to strengthen its Welsh policy. In the 1992 election Labour's policy had been to establish a Welsh regional council – and 'regional' was the significant word. This would have the same status as the regional councils it proposed to establish in England in its fifth year of government. Its Scottish and Welsh policies were thoroughly reconsidered after 1992. It resurrected the Kilbrandon Commission recommendations of 1973. Scotland, where the SNP threat to the Labour Party was then far greater than the Plaid Cymru threat in Wales, was to have a legislative parliament, whereas Wales would have a national assembly which would take over the powers of the Welsh Office.

Wales and the European Union

Plaid Cymru had for years emphasised the importance of a strong Welsh representation in the European Union whose new decentralist regionalism it found most attractive. It urged the creation of a Welsh Embassy in Brussels to further strengthen the splendid WEA, but lacked the political weight, or even a member in the European Parliament, to press the matter home. It was active within the League of representatives of small nations and historic regions, in which Jill Evans and Eurig Wyn were prominent. The League had fifteen members of the European Parliament, now joined by Jill and Eurig. When Eurig became one of the three British members of the EU's Regional Committee in Brussels, the first time for Wales to be represented on a body which was an organic part of the EU, Jill Evans was his deputy.

Plaid's ultimate goal was full Welsh membership in the EU. Under the renewed presidency of Dafydd Wigley the party fought for a legislative parliament which would ensure a close relationship between Wales and Brussels. Opponents of full membership jeered at the idea, contending that Wales gets far more Union help with the weight of Great Britain behind it. The hollowness of this claim has often been exposed in the experience of Wales, and recent evidence from Ireland, whose population is similar to ours, discloses its glaring untruth.

Ireland had been a desperately poor country in my lifetime, so poor that it was constantly used to warn the Welsh against the danger of self-government. I have vivid memories of barefooted children in the streets of Dublin. As recently as 1956 the Welsh gross national product was nearly twice that of Ireland. But since 1987, 337,000 new jobs have been created in Ireland while its income per head exceeds that of England and is far greater than that of Wales. John Osmond says that the staggering success of Ireland is largely due to three external factors. The three are the result of self-government. The first is the flow of inward investment; the second is Irish response to the world trading environment, and the third is the use Irish government has made of autonomous representation in Brussels from 1989, when it gained the vitally important Objective One status, onwards. In 1987 Ireland's net receipts from the European Union were £1.7 billion. In face of such facts the contentions of the opponents of membership of the European Union are laughable.

Labour Party Members Warm to Wales

Apart from the growth of Plaid Cymru the most encouraging development in Welsh politics during the last decade has been the growth of the number of Labour Party members who sincerely want to create the conditions of a full national life for Wales. Although Mrs Thatcher must be thanked for much of this change, a far more fundamental cause is the growing sense of national identity. Their leader when he was shadow Secretary of State for Wales and afterwards the Secretary in the Cabinet, was Ron Davies, described by Dafydd Wigley as Welsh Labour to distinguish him from New Labour and Old Labour. These Labour members renounced Labour centralism and tended to favour a legislative parliament for Wales. No fewer than thirteen Welsh Labour MPs signed an early day motion in 1989 in favour of a parliament for Wales. London Labour leaders were unitedly opposed, although supporting a legislative parliament for Scotland. They declared that unlike 1979 there would be no referendum. This was emphasised by Ron Davies three days before Tony Blair announced that he had changed his mind; London had decided that there would be a referendum after all. Plaid Cymru demanded that if there was to be a referendum it should enable the Welsh people to have a fair choice between three possibilities, the status quo, an elected parliament with limited powers and full self-government within the European Union.

The Labour Party finally approved its plan for a non-legislative Assembly for Wales and a legislative Parliament for Scotland early in 1997. Although parity with Scotland was Plaid Cymru's policy it avoided attacking the plan, only calling for more

The final result of the vote on a National Assembly for Wales is declared in Cardiff (photograph: Keith Morris)

powers. After ensuring that there would be no repetition of the bitter 1979 experience it cooperated fully with the Labour Party. Many of its members supported the non-party 'Yes for Wales' campaign, which performed an invaluable service, but the party carefully avoided taking the high ground. The plan was Labour's and had to be seen so. Ron Davies was the able and determined leader who won the day. It required courage to lead from the front, insisting as he did that devolution was a process, not an event. It is not too much to say that without his resolute enthusiasm there would be no Assembly on Welsh soil today. But the price he paid for his courage and vision was his malicious expulsion from a series of responsible posts.

Although Plaid Cymru thought the Assembly was less than necessary, it fought as a united party. This could not be said of the Labour Party. True, it suffered from nothing like the depth of its

1979 divisions, yet there were a number of prominent dissident Labour MPs and a number not so prominent, such as Dr Alan Williams, MP for Carmarthen. There were also numerous dissident Labour councillors from Cardiff to Holyhead. Although Neil Kinnock, leader of the 1979 fatal opposition, did not oppose publicly, neither did he give an hour's active support. Privately he declared that his opposition was even stronger than it was two decades before. From the Welsh standpoint the Labour Party is incomparably healthier than it was decades ago. There is no one in office to compare with George Thomas, an open enemy of decentralisation of power and of the Welsh language.

Conservatives led the 'No to Wales' movement with the aid of a few eccentrics. Their attitude continued to be dismally negative, indicating the need for a truly Welsh Conservative party working for a positive Welsh policy.

It was clear to all who cooperated to secure an elected national political institution that they were facing a tremendous challenge. Who could forget that only two decades had passed since a similar proposal was thrown back in the government's teeth by a humiliating majority of four to one? Since then there had clearly been some growth in self-respect and self-confidence, but whether it would prove to be enough to bung the enormous 1979 gap was an open question to say the least. In these circumstances to secure a positive referendum majority, very small though it was, could be hailed as a notable historic victory, by far the most important event in Welsh political history. The referendum was followed by the dramatic resignation of Ron Davies from the post of Welsh Secretary of State, and then the leadership of the Labour Party in Wales and the Assembly's First Secretary. Alun Michael was appointed Secretary of State and he was Blair's choice in the election of First Secretary and leader of the Assembly. Rhodri Morgan, the other candidate, won a substantial majority of votes, but in the Millbank-rigged election by a so-called electoral college, Michael was undemocratically elected leader of the Labour Party in Wales and consequently leader of the National Assembly. The event would have profound repercussions.

A Quiet Revolution

The ensuing Assembly elections held on the tenth of May shook the land. A number of the heavy dailies described it as the heaviest blow yet suffered by Tony Blair. Before the election, few outside Plaid Cymru would have been surprised if Labour had won the election with the kind of overwhelming majority it had enjoyed for generations in the Westminster elections. In fact, it failed even to achieve a majority. It was Plaid Cymru which now set the agenda.

Among the first seats won by Plaid Cymru were three in which the Labour majority used to be counted in tens of thousands. The first to fall was Neil Kinnock's former seat, Islwyn, followed by Rhondda and Llanelli. Three other seats in which it did remarkably well were West Carmarthen and South Pembrokeshire, where Labour's majority was only 492, Cwm Cynon where it was 672 and Pontypridd where it was 5%. Even Ron Davies's majority over Plaid Cymru in Caerffili was only 10%. Most impressive also was the pervasive nature of Plaid's growth throughout Wales. The immense contribution made to the party's success by Dafydd Wigley's inspiring leadership must be noted.

Welsh Assembly

	First vote		Second vote		Total seats
	Seats	%	Seats	%	
Labour	27	39	1	39	28
Plaid Cymru	9	27	8	28	17
Conservative	1	16	8	15	9
Lib Dem	3	12	3	13	6

Scottish Parliament

	First vote		Second vote		Total seats
	Seats	%	Seats	%	
Labour	53	39	3	33	56
SNP	7	29	28	28	35
Conservative	0	16	18	16	18
Lib Dem	12	14	17	16	17
Others	1	3	2	6	3

Council Elections in the UK

Party	Total councils	Change in control	Seats won	Net change in seats
Conservative	61	+48	3,762	+1,345
Labour	138	-32	4,803	-1,145
Lib Dem	20	-11	2,611	-88
Plaid Cymru	3	+2	205	+82
SNP	1	-2	205	+14
Green			25	+14

European Elections in Wales

Party	Total Vote	Percentage of votes	Seats
Labour	200,688	31.95	22
Plaid Cymru	185,235	28.86	10
Conservative	142,831	22.71	8
Lib Dem	51,073	8.76	–

Distribution of European Parliament seats:
Labour – 2; Plaid Cymru – 2; Conservative – 1

The Range of Plaid Cymru's Success

The great increase in support for the freedom movement was reflected in Plaid Cymru's successes in the County Council and the European Parliament elections. The party broke Labour's monopoly in the industrial valleys by winning control of the Rhondda and Caerffili councils in addition to Gwynedd. The 205 council seats which it won equalled the total won by the SNP in Scotland.

Whereas in the 1995 European election the Labour Party won all five Welsh seats, in 1999 it held only two. Plaid Cymru won two and the Tories one. The membership of Jill Evans and Eurig Wyn in the EU parliament, where they joined the large Green group, makes Welsh action free of London control possible for the first time. No doubt they will form a close relationship with the fifteen-strong Irish contingent. It is essential that the National Assembly gives the EU high priority. An immediate need is the designation of an Assembly minister as Secretary for Europe. Plaid's electoral successes indicate the extent of the growth in the sense of Welsh national identity.

While Plaid Cymru's performance was its best ever, Labour's in contrast was its worst since 1918, while the Conservatives sank lower than in any previous election. By coming within 2% of Labour's overall vote, Plaid shattered Labour's long-standing domination and denied it the overall majority which it had taken for granted. It has wisely sought to cooperate with the minority government wherever possible.

On the Threshold of National Freedom

There was some confusion in the minority Labour government of the National Assembly in its opening months in consequence of the undemocratic election of Alun Michael as First Secretary.

By far the most important issue facing the Assembly was the European Union Objective One funds, which had contributed so much to the creation of the Irish tiger economy in a small country which had been far poorer than Wales, but in which 337,000 new jobs had been created in just over a decade. The grant of Objective One funding depended however on securing matching funds from the London Treasury. This presented no serious difficulty to self-governing Ireland, but getting support from the London Treasury was a different story. In Plaid Cymru's 1999 conference Dafydd Wigley warned the Assembly that Plaid Cymru would present a vote of no confidence in Alun Michael unless he fought successfully for the matching funds. As Labour's Assembly budget months later contained no matching funds from the Treasury, the lack of confidence motion went ahead. Alun Michael was compelled to resign, and as he had too little support in the Labour Party to be re-elected, he was replaced by Rhodri Morgan.

This democratic victory, which strengthened the Assembly, was endorsed when Plaid Cymru's Simon Thomas won a splendid by-election victory in Ceredigion in which Labour was pushed into third place. It will soon be further strengthened by gaining the power of primary legislation for which there is a considerable majority.

Throughout her long history Cymru has fought with her back to the wall without certainty of survival. Today we live in an unusually hopeful period. There is confidence that our nation will live, that Cymru has a national future and that her great potential will be realised. The day of national freedom is dawning.